Cambridge Elements

Elements in Environmental Humanities
edited by
Louise Westling
University of Oregon
Serenella Iovino
University of North Carolina at Chapel Hill
Timo Maran
University of Tartu

AUTOMOBILITY AND THE ANTHROPOCENE

The Car as Post-Human

Gordon M. Sayre
University of Oregon

Shaftesbury Road, Cambridge CB2 8EA, United Kingdom

One Liberty Plaza, 20th Floor, New York, NY 10006, USA

477 Williamstown Road, Port Melbourne, VIC 3207, Australia

314–321, 3rd Floor, Plot 3, Splendor Forum, Jasola District Centre,
New Delhi – 110025, India

103 Penang Road, #05–06/07, Visioncrest Commercial, Singapore 238467

Cambridge University Press is part of Cambridge University Press & Assessment,
a department of the University of Cambridge.

We share the University's mission to contribute to society through the pursuit of
education, learning and research at the highest international levels of excellence.

www.cambridge.org
Information on this title: www.cambridge.org/9781009526746

DOI: 10.1017/9781009526715

© Gordon M. Sayre 2025

This publication is in copyright. Subject to statutory exception and to the provisions
of relevant collective licensing agreements, no reproduction of any part may take
place without the written permission of Cambridge University Press & Assessment.

When citing this work, please include a reference to the DOI 10.1017/9781009526715

First published 2025

A catalogue record for this publication is available from the British Library

ISBN 978-1-009-52674-6 Hardback
ISBN 978-1-009-52673-9 Paperback
ISSN 2632-3125 (online)
ISSN 2632-3117 (print)

Cambridge University Press & Assessment has no responsibility for the persistence
or accuracy of URLs for external or third-party internet websites referred to in this
publication and does not guarantee that any content on such websites is, or will remain,
accurate or appropriate.

For EU product safety concerns, contact us at Calle de José Abascal, 56, 1°, 28003
Madrid, Spain, or email eugpsr@cambridge.org

Automobility and the Anthropocene

The Car as Post-Human

Elements in Environmental Humanities

DOI: 10.1017/9781009526715
First published online: June 2025

Gordon M. Sayre
University of Oregon

Author for correspondence: Gordon M. Sayre, gsayre@uoregon.edu

Abstract: The automobile has transformed Earth's habitats and humans' habits since the 1890s, when it, this Element argues, began the Anthropocene. Climate change now motivates efforts to reduce greenhouse gas emissions, of which cars and trucks account for at least 10 percent. Shifting to electric vehicles is not enough; one needs to better understand the power cars hold over humans. Environmental humanities scholars examine human/machine hybrids but have ignored the most obvious example: humans driving cars are social agents constituting a civil society of automobility in roadscape environments. This Element traces the evolution of cars from horsecars, carriages, and bicycles, and the influence of Henry Ford and Alfred P. Sloan on labor standards and consumer behaviors. As the car industry pushes high-tech autonomous or self-driving vehicles, it relies on futuristic fantasies and false promises. The ills of automobility cannot be solved with new products that only intensify human dependence on cars.

Keywords: automobility, Anthropocene, post-humanism, car-driver, cars

© Gordon M. Sayre 2025

ISBNs: 9781009526746 (HB), 9781009526739 (PB), 9781009526715 (OC)
ISSNs: 2632-3125 (online), 2632-3117 (print)

Contents

Introduction	1
1 Cars in Twentieth-Century Social Theory and Twenty-First-Century Post-Humanism	5
2 Cars and the Anthropocene	21
3 Cars, Futurism, and Nostalgia	36
4 Carbolization	51
References	65

Introduction

Earth faces grave dangers from a warming climate, exacerbated by anthropogenic greenhouse gas (GHG) emissions. Data collected by the Intergovernmental Panel on Climate Change for 2019 show that 15 percent of direct emissions were from transport, of which two-thirds were from road transport: cars and trucks. In North America, the proportion is much higher; roughly 30 percent of emissions are from transport (Parmesan et al., 2022). In California – the epicenter of the postindustrial global information economy and (as we will see in Section 4) the birthplace of automotive emissions regulation – the share of emissions from cars and trucks is even higher. Governor Gavin Newsom acknowledged: "the transportation sector is responsible for more than half of all of California's carbon pollution, 80 percent of smog-forming pollution and 95 percent of toxic diesel emissions." In response to the problem, Newsom announced in September 2020 a plan to "develop regulations to mandate that 100 percent of in-state sales of new passenger cars and trucks are zero-emission by 2035 – a target which would achieve more than a 35 percent reduction in greenhouse gas emissions and an 80 percent improvement in oxides of nitrogen emissions from cars statewide" (Newsom, 2020). Will it prove possible to enforce this ban on new gasoline and diesel vehicles? Reader, please update yourself on California's progress toward meeting that 2035 deadline.

Regulating and reducing automobile tailpipe emissions is necessary to limit catastrophic climate change, but controlling these emissions cannot be achieved solely through technical innovations – in this case, ubiquitous new electric cars (and the network of charging stations required to keep them moving). Newsom, former President Biden, environmental and climate activists, as well as auto industry executives like Elon Musk, have all invoked techno-futurism to make such ambitious mandates and grand promises seem plausible. Engineering historian Peter Norton has described the techno-futurism that infests Americans and their cars with the term *Autonorama*: "lavish promises are made: traffic congestion will be eliminated, collisions will cease, efficiency gains will reduce waste and pollution ... new technology is just like magic" (Norton, 2021: 15). This sense of magic is familiar from advertising campaigns; the consumer can solve problems simply by purchasing a new product – in this case, a car. No change in habit or instinct will be required. Other sectors of climate change policy often rely on similar magic: invent a technical fix; claim it will solve a serious problem; and ignore the practical, behavioral, and infrastructural work required to apply the new technology and meet the ambitious goal. Then repeat the cycle with a new gadget and new promise. Many people interpret these pronouncements as a license to continue their wasteful, polluting, or dangerous behaviors. With respect to California's zero-emission cars mandate, just a decade away as I write, the task becomes even more implausible given the fact that nearly every consumer who buys a new electric car will sell their internal combustion car to another driver, in California or elsewhere. On a global scale, older cars that are sold (and some that are stolen) in the affluent, regulated markets of North America, Europe, and Japan are often shipped to the poorer, less regulated developing world. Hence even if policymakers believe they are replacing polluting cars with cleaner cars, they are not really doing so with respect to global GHG emissions. And what of the California consumers who are happy with their internal combustion cars and don't want to buy an electric car? The mandate does not explicitly state the rate at which regulators expect the enormous fleet of California cars and trucks to be transformed, before or after 2035.

Significantly reducing GHG emissions requires actions that affect the entire fleet, not only new cars, and necessitates changing the behaviors of all car-drivers, not just early adopters of a trendy technology or product. Car-drivers' behavior is cultural and political; it involves the history of automobiles and roadscapes, and it is a product of drivers' emotional relationships with their cars. Policy measures such as Newsom's decree are techno-futurist and ignore the behavior and attitudes of consumers – in this case, car-drivers. A very brief survey of automobile emissions, safety, and emissions regulation in the United States can put this into context.

Beginning in the early 1960s, the US Congress and President Lyndon Johnson reacted to severe air quality problems, especially in Southern California, as well as the research and testimony of Ralph Nader and the success of his book *Unsafe at Any Speed*. They drew up legislation to place responsibility upon manufacturers to change their cars. Driver behavior did not need to change. First came the Clean Air Act in 1963, prompted in part by the activism of California politicians who forced Detroit manufacturers to install positive crankcase ventilation or PCV valves on new cars to reduce smog. The National Traffic and Motor Vehicle Safety Act, passed in the summer of 1966, obliged manufacturers to fit all new cars with headrests, energy-absorbing steering wheels, shatter-resistant windshields, and seat belts (though laws requiring drivers and passengers to wear seat belts did not begin until the 1980s). In 1970, the National Environmental Policy Act and significant amendments to the Clean Air Act imposed goals for improving air quality and reducing harmful emissions from car engines. The catalytic converter was the most important engineering innovation for reducing smog. After the Arab oil embargo of 1973–74, the Environmental Protection Agency (EPA), created in 1970, was also tasked with writing regulations to improve vehicle fuel efficiency. The primary policy tool the EPA applied was corporate average fuel economy or CAFÉ standards, which require car manufacturers marketing vehicles in the United States to meet a fuel economy threshold for the entire fleet of cars and light trucks they sell each year. The bureaucratic details of this history are complex, and we will expand on some key aspects of this story in Section 4. The takeaway is that in all three forms of automotive externalities: crash safety, pollution control, and fuel efficiency, mandates were placed on carmakers to redesign and reengineer the products they sold. Consumers were not obliged to modify older cars they already owned, and drivers and passengers were not forced to drive less or to drive more safely. Consequently, improvements in road safety, air quality, and resource conservation in the United States have been gradual and fragile, subject to abrupt changes, as has occurred with the Obama, Trump, and Biden administrations. The rate of annual fatalities from car crashes has increased since 2020, and vehicle miles traveled (VMT) have continued to rise as well (NHTSA, 2024).

To seriously reduce GHG emissions that cause climate change, the consumerist approach that has worked for more than sixty years will no longer suffice. Electric vehicles have been promoted as a replacement for internal combustion engines, an engineering marvel as effective as airbags and catalytic converters, but EVs are not magic. The sources needed to generate the additional electricity required to power a huge new fleet of vehicles are not yet available on the electric grid. Using fossil fuels to generate this electricity might represent a smaller amount of GHG emissions than burning gasoline and diesel to power existing cars (because electric motors are inherently more efficient), but obtaining the new resources – notably lithium, copper, and cobalt – required for so many electric cars will cause severe environmental impacts from new mines. In the face of this technological and political uncertainty, the global car industry now suffers from tremendous overcapacity, especially in China. China's (and the rest of the world's) cheap cars, redundant factories, and overbuilt highways also constitute significant environmental harms. So how can the environmental problem of cars best be addressed, or even comprehended?

This Element reaches back to the late nineteenth century, to the introduction of the car as a mass consumer product, to examine how early cars replaced horse-drawn carriages and wagons. The horse-drawn carriage was a costly status symbol. Early automobiles were marketed using images and terminology associated with carriages, and some of these terms endured for decades. Cars supplanted both the carriages and wagons, as well as the living beings that had carried humans and their belongings for millennia, and cars were anthropomorphized in some of the same ways. The car-driver today is a descendant of those interspecies hybrid entities, and cars have taken on many humanistic traits.

I try to follow a reciprocal, systemic methodology. The Anthropocene is a concept of the earth-system, which entails the study of Earth and atmospheric cycles of water, carbon, nitrates, aerosols, and other substances. Each system, and each organism within it, has inputs and outputs, and the same applies to people or car-drivers. The system of automobility is all-encompassing in modern life because nearly every human drives, owns, or rides in cars. Hardly anyone can opt out of automobility, honestly deny, or feasibly escape their complicity in it, just as no one can avoid contributing to or suffering from anthropogenic climate change. Postures of purity and self-denial are pointless, and contradictions between doctrine and practice are inevitable. Americans, in general, too often admonish others without changing their own behavior, whether with respect to health and exercise, sexuality, household finance, racial politics, and so on. Regarding cars, such hypocrisy is also pervasive. Given the circumstances, theory and practice cannot be separated in this study of cars and automobility. Every worker or producer is also a consumer, though not every car-driver works in an automobile factory. Every car-driver who contributes to the external costs or externalities of automobility, such as air pollution, GHG emissions, and resource depletion, also suffers to some degree from these effects (Porter, 1999). And nearly every scholar who contributes to the academic discourse of environmental humanities is or was also a car-driver, so their habits as car-drivers are relevant to understanding their writings.

My inspiration to study automobility and the Anthropocene stems from a lifelong fascination with car design and marketing, as well as from teaching an undergraduate course in Folklore at the University of Oregon, entitled "Car Cultures," since 2010. As a scholar and teacher of environmental humanities, I have often wondered why cars have not received the attention they deserve from my academic colleagues, despite the widely known and discussed environmental problems and threats outlined above. I aim for this Element to remain relevant in ten years, so I have chosen not to include tables of statistics, and my policy predictions and prescriptions are intentionally limited. Instead, I focus on the persistence of early patterns in car design and on debunking claims that cars are high-tech and the bearers of futurity. Much of this history centers on the United States, both because it is where I live and follow automotive and regulatory news, and because the United States – particularly California – has established regulatory patterns for automobility that have since influenced other parts of the world.

1 Cars in Twentieth-Century Social Theory and Twenty-First-Century Post-Humanism

1.1 Antonio Gramsci on Fordism, Theodor Adorno on Sloanism

In the twentieth century, prominent social theorists were strongly influenced by capitalists' promotion of, and Marxists' responses to, the rise of the auto industry. Henry Ford's success with the Model T, the first car marketed toward rural and working classes, inspired both Vladimir Lenin and Adolf Hitler, as well as other heads of state who wanted to modernize and enrich their nations. Fordism became a buzzword shortly after the publication of Henry Ford's *My Life and Work* in 1922, and although it was used with varying meanings, Fordism remained relevant into the 1980s when the declining market share of Ford, General Motors, and Chrysler, and the rise of Toyota and other Japanese manufacturers in the US market, prompted business and academic leaders to promote flexible or just-in-time manufacturing as a post-Fordism that would change working conditions, labor-management relations, and political economy on a global scale. David Harvey's *The Condition of Postmodernity* is among the most respected studies of late capitalism, and yet Harvey mentions Fordism and the auto industry only briefly (Harvey, 1990: 128, 134).

Sloanism, a term for the business and marketing philosophies of Alfred P. Sloan, who led General Motors Corporation (hereafter "GM") from the early 1920s until 1956, is less commonly used than Fordism outside the car industry but is equally important for marketing and consumerism, wherein the car is the essential product to which consumers devote their money, mobility, safety, self-image, and livelihood. The tensions between Fordism and Sloanism in US politics, business, and law gave rise to consumerism, a mindset far broader than cars and automobility but one that combines odd precepts. The driver is at once ultimately responsible for their car (think insurance and liability) and yet indemnified for the car's failings (think emissions and product recalls), at once deeply invested in their car (for emotional and social status) and eternally dissatisfied with the car's shortcomings (due to the planned obsolescence that motivates the purchase of another car). GM's head of research, Charles Kettering, published an article in 1926 titled "Keep the Customer Dissatisfied," which insisted on planned obsolescence because "If everyone were satisfied, no one would buy the new thing" (qtd. in Norton, 25).

Let's begin by explaining how Fordism and Sloanism can help interpret Marxist social theory and how they prepared for post-humanist theory. Economists have long focused on the car industry to a degree disproportionate to its true share of employment and productivity. As political scientist Mathew Paterson writes: "the car industry is often taken as a paradigm case of a globalized industry ... this literature in general assumes the centrality of the car industry to national economic success" (Paterson, 2007: 98, 101). We will see in Section 4 how Korea and then China set out to replicate the success Japan had enjoyed starting in the 1970s by using automobile exports to grow into a global industrial leader. By contrast, experts in business and political economy, as well as scholars working in literature, philosophy, anthropology, and sociology – even those using Marxist methodologies – often ignore or misinterpret cars and the car industry. A pair of British sociologists wrote at the end of the twentieth century: "in contrast to other culturally-transforming technologies, notably mass television and electronic information processing, the apparently irresistible rise of the car has gone virtually unnoticed by sociologists" (Dant & Martin, 2001). Humanist social theorists also generally ignored cars, but a pair of philosophers who did write about the industry were influenced by the doctrines of Fordism and Sloanism.

The work of Antonio Gramsci and Theodor Adorno can help unravel Marxist social theory and the car industry in the twentieth century. Gramsci studied at the University of Turin, and his career as a journalist for socialist newspapers, a labor organizer, and a politician grew at the same time as car manufacturing was making Turin the Detroit of Italy. Fiat and Lancia, both based in Turin, implemented Fordist techniques earlier than other European carmakers (Harvey, 1990: 128), and Gramsci responded by helping strategize for labor unions there until he was arrested by Benito Mussolini's henchmen and spent the rest of his life in prison, from 1926 to 1937. The notebooks Gramsci wrote by hand while incarcerated, more than thirty of them, are the corpus that secured his fame as a philosopher. In one of them, he defined Fordism as:

> ... the experiments conducted by Ford and to the economies made by his firm through direct management of transport and distribution of the product. These economies affected production costs and permitted higher wages and lower selling prices. ... [I]t was relatively easy to rationalise production and labour by a skilful combination of force (destruction of working-class trade unionism on a territorial basis) and persuasion (high wages, various social benefits, extremely subtle ideological and political propaganda) and thus succeed in making the whole life of the nation revolve around production. (Gramsci, 1971: 570–571)

Henry Ford's 1922 memoir *My Life and Work*, co-authored with (or ghostwritten by) Samuel Crowther, was among the few books Gramsci had in prison, and it was also read eagerly by Vladimir Lenin and Adolf Hitler. That both murderous despots were starstruck by Ford, and both invited him to visit their countries and invest in factories and joint ventures, suggests how much their rival ideologies overlapped. Ford's antisemitism, which he (or Crowther) defended near the end of the book, likely also appealed to Hitler and Lenin

(250–252). Between 1923 and 1933, twenty-nine editions of Ford's propaganda tract *The International Jew* were published in translation in Germany, and Hitler also declared, "the motorcar, instead of being a class-dividing element, can be the instrument for uniting the different classes, just as it has done in America, thanks to Mr. Ford's genius" (qtd. in Flink, 1988: 113). Lenin opposed the Taylorization of labor before the Russian Revolution but quickly embraced it afterward, when he accused Russian workers of being lazy and unproductive (Settis, 2019: 378–379). The car factory, and especially Ford's Detroit factories, became emblematic of the industrial proletariat and of labor union organizing, from the famous "Five Dollar Day" instituted at Highland Park in Dearborn in 1914 to the River Rouge plant Ford Motor Company began to build in 1927, which became the largest factory in the world. Still today, the United Auto Workers union and its contracts with the Detroit 3 carmakers – Ford, GM, and the former Chrysler (now part of Stellantis) – set the standards for negotiations with other large unions. However, industrial policies long ago diverged from the man and the company that had inspired political propagandists and social theorists. According to one Gramsci scholar:

> Gramsci's Fordism no longer existed by the time he was writing about it: the Five Dollar Day had been eroded by massive inflation during the war and then dismantled in 1920; Ford factories underwent a deep restructuring in 1927 to catch up with General Motors; the 1929 crisis had crushed the whole model of consumption and exports; in the 1930s Ford was forced to face the increasing role of Big Labour in politics and Big Government in the economy – namely, the New Deal. (Settis, 2019: 386)

The success of Ford and Fordism was not achieved only on the factory floor; it was made possible by the mass migration of laborers to the Detroit area, both from Europe and from the US South. The reason "mass-production techniques came to be innovated in the United States is that, in contrast with Europe, automobile manufacturers here could count on the availability of a large labor pool of unskilled, recently arrived, and as yet politically impotent peasants from the most socially and economically backward countries of Europe, and of blacks escaping ... from the rural American South" (Flink, 1988: 118). Such mass migration is also characteristic of the global Anthropocene, as we will see in Section 4. A neocolonial Fordism, rarely referred to by that name, has followed the growth of the car industry in Asia and around the world.

Misconceptions about Fordism are further evidence that car manufacturing still plays an outsized role in global political economy, as well as in industrial and trade policy, because virtually all political factions share an awareness of cars, either as consumers/drivers or, in some cases, as workers. People who neither write about nor even know much about Fordism nonetheless repeat the myth that Henry Ford invented the assembly line. Charles E. Sorensen was one of several key engineers and managers at Ford who implemented the production techniques later referred to as Fordist: "In later years he [Henry Ford] was glorified as the originator of the mass production idea. Far from it; he just grew into it, like the rest of us" (Sorensen & Williamson, 1956: 128). Sorensen claims, "I installed the first conveyor system" to deliver various parts assemblies to the main-level assembly line, and: "Years later, in *My Life and Work*, a book that was written for him, Mr. Ford said that the conveyor-assembly idea occurred to him after watching the reverse process in packing houses, where hogs and steers were triced up by hind legs on an overhead conveyer and disassembled. This is a rationalization [...] Mr. Ford had nothing to do with originating, planning, and carrying-out the assembly line" (129). Ford was a genius at self-promotion, so long as he had assistance from Crowther and from William J. Cameron, editor of *The Dearborn Independent*, Ford's main outlet for antisemitism and political commentary. But most who are critical of Fordism, as well as all those in favor, continue to blame or credit Henry for it.

Recent research in political economy cuts through these myths. Capitalism, in this view, suffers from chronic overproduction because firms try to maximize profits by reducing labor costs and increasing productivity, even though they "need wages to rise to facilitate consumption of the industry's products" (Paterson, 2007: 104). One of the most enduring aspects of Fordist theory is to perceive how this overproduction, or "regime of accumulation," to use a term favored by Marxists, demanded or provoked a regime of regulation, such as labor laws, workplace safety codes, and trade policies, that try to protect both the auto industry and its workers. In the estimation of Settis, these regulatory frameworks ended Fordism roughly a decade after it began. But Paterson defines the term differently: "It was struggles in the car industry above all which had produced by 1945 the key elements in the Fordist class compromise involving the recognition of union rights, full employment policies, the family wage principle underlying wage rates" (108). Crowther and Ford articulated the third principle in a subsequent book: "The right wage is the highest wage the employer can steadily pay. That is where the ingenuity of the employer comes in. He has to create customers, and if he is making a commodity, then his own workers are among his best customers" (Ford, 1926: 155). In this broader sense, Fordism associates the worldwide industrial and economic boom from the late 1920s until the early 1970s with the car industry and with a US economy that was heavily dependent on cars. Leading cultural theorists of the 1980s and 1990s, such as Harvey, Frederic Jameson, and Paul Gilroy, analyzed this process as post-Fordism, although a broader group of intellectuals (since most of them weren't interested in cars) called it postmodernism.

Alfred P. Sloan began working at GM with the assignment of catching up to Ford Motor's Model T, which in 1918 amounted to around half the cars on the road in the United States. In 1926, Sloan appealed to Lawrence Fisher, whom he had hired to lead the Cadillac division of GM, to find a designer to style a new model named LaSalle. Fisher had started a coach-building business along with his brothers in 1908, producing car bodies for clients who purchased the chassis and drivetrain separately, as was common for high-end cars well into the 1930s. Harley Earl's family had also been coachbuilders, based in Southern California, doing custom coachwork for Hollywood stars including Mary Pickford, Tom Mix, Cecil B. DeMille, and Roscoe "Fatty" Arbuckle. Sloan saw that his company might outsell Ford if it countered the boxy, utilitarian, price-cutting esthetics of the Model T with more sleek and attractive cars, and Earl quickly obliged by designing the longer, lower LaSalle model. Sloan wrote in a memo: "I think the future of General Motors will be measured by the attractiveness that we put into the bodies from the standpoint of luxury of appointment, the degree to which they please the eye both in contour and in color scheme, also the degree to which we are able to make them different from competition" (Farber, 2002: 102). GM soon became the largest buyer of magazine advertising in the nation, while also expanding its financing division to entice customers to buy new cars on the installment plan. In 1927, Ford, after steadily cutting prices for the Model T and beginning to lose market share, was forced to shut down factories and retool them to produce the more esthetically pleasing Model A, which would compete with GM's Chevrolet as well as a range of other makes. Sloan had arranged GM around five divisions, assembled by William Durant from among the many brands Durant had bought out over the previous decade as they had been outdistanced by Ford. Chevrolet, Oakland (renamed Pontiac in 1931), Oldsmobile, Buick, and Cadillac formed a brand hierarchy from mass-market to elite luxury, even as the design, engineering, and manufacturing of the drivetrains were managed collectively by GM. Sloanism emphasized form over function, design over manufacturing, finance over engineering, and planned obsolescence over the Model T's puritanical insistence on reliability, consistency, and a driver's ability to do roadside repairs, as all motorists had to do in the pre–World War I era.

Critical theory's response to Sloanism came from Theodor Adorno, a German Jewish émigré philosopher who lived and worked in Los Angeles from 1941 to 1949, where he and his wife drove a Plymouth (Jenemann, 2007: 157). He was among the most influential twentieth-century philosophers of art and esthetics. His writings from the period reflect harshly upon American film, music, and literature as mass-market commodities produced by monopolistic firms. Occasionally, Adorno wrote a few lines about the most expensive, sought-after products in America, cars:

> That the difference between the Chrysler range and General Motors products is basically illusory strikes every child with a keen interest in varieties. What connoisseurs discuss as good or bad points serve only to perpetuate the semblance of competition and range of choice. The same applies to the Warner Brothers and Metro Goldwyn Mayer productions. (Adorno & Horkheimer, 1944: 123).

Adorno was a classical musician and a nostalgic esthete, reacting to industrial modernity in an emotional, sentimental way, even as he did not resist it in a theoretical way, given his Marxist belief in teleological progress. "Culture industry," the term coined by Adorno and his co-author Max Horkheimer, explains how artistic productions: "hit songs, stars, and soap operas," and the "gags, effects, and jokes" they employ, become predictable, standardized, interchangeable parts, like those assembled by auto workers into a Chrysler or Cadillac. In a later work, Adorno commented on these parts:

> While a Cadillac undoubtedly excels a Chevrolet by the amount that it costs more, this superiority, unlike that of the old Rolls Royce, nevertheless itself proceeds from an overall plan which artfully equips the former with the better cylinders, the latter with the worse cylinders, bolts, accessories, without anything being altered in the basic pattern of the mass-produced article; only minor rearrangements in production would be needed to turn the Chevrolet into a Cadillac. So luxury is sapped. (Adorno, 1951: Aphorism #77)

Adorno misinterpreted Sloanism. The cylinders and bolts in the Cadillac were no better than those in the Chevrolet. It was not the functional drivetrain so much as the exterior styling, for instance, the tailfins, that General Motors used to justify the higher price of the Cadillac. One wonders if Adorno had seen or learned about any of the custom coach-built cars designed by Harley Earl's family firm in Hollywood; he might have approved of their luxury. It appears he did not, because the sentence immediately preceding those two reads: "As per Veblen's theory, it is more about permitting those who can pay, to prove to themselves and others their status, than about meeting their, in any case, increasingly undifferentiated needs" (Adorno, 1951; Veblen, 1899). Adorno believed in an aristocracy of taste that offered a life of "luxury" and distinction to an educated elite, but not to the masses. He also held false assumptions about how machine modernity changed creativity, and, unlike Sloan, saw variety and ephemerality as inimical to quality and progress. Adorno's essay "On Popular Music" is among his most widely read works because its harsh comments on jazz have provoked scholars of American rock and roll and pop, genres of the 1950s to 1990s that they see as heirs to Adorno's "jazz" in the 1940s. Adorno doubted that jazz musicians truly improvised, "The most drastic example of standardization of presumably individualized features is to be found in so-called improvisations. Even though jazz musicians still improvise in practice, their improvisations have become so normalized" (Adorno, 1941: 25). In an essay titled "Theodor Adorno Meets the Cadillacs," Theodore Gendron critiques Adorno's confusion between pseudo-individualization, such as the stylistic differences between Chevrolet and Cadillac, or a jazz soloist's improvisation on a pop song's melody, and part-interchangeability, an essential principle of the automobile factory but merely a structural metaphor for musical patterns. In Section 3, we will see how popular musicians writing songs about cars, especially music stars who had worked in car factories, understood these differences much better than cultural studies scholars.

The automobile industry epitomized industrial capitalism in the twentieth century. Theories of how art and culture changed as a consequence of industrial capitalism understandably looked to cars and carmakers for evidence, but their conclusions were often wrong. Corporate titans like Henry Ford and Alfred P. Sloan were ascribed with genius properly reserved for artists, while myriad car-drivers, who saw the failings of the carmakers and worked to reshape commodity vehicles into things of beauty, were not recognized for their esthetic talents.

The most trenchant Marxist analysis of Fordism was one of the simplest. A key debate for twentieth-century social theorists was between those (including both Fascists and Marxists who admired Henry Ford) who saw the car as the vehicle of Fordist modernity and prosperity, bringing affluence to the masses, and a dissenting strain, including Theodor Adorno and André Gorz, who saw cars as an exclusive luxury. André Gorz was the nom de plume of Austrian Gerhart Hirsch, born in 1923, who fled to Switzerland to avoid conscription into the Wehrmacht. After the war, he moved to Paris and became a friend of Jean-Paul Sartre, Herbert Marcuse, and Ivan Illich, as well as a successful leftist journalist, editor, and public intellectual. His brief essay "l'Idéologie sociale de la bagnole," or "The Social Ideology of the Car," begins by debunking the Fordist doctrine that car ownership should be an egalitarian ideal:

> The worst thing about cars is that they are like castles or villas by the sea ... Unlike the vacuum cleaner, the radio, or the bicycle, which retain their use value when everyone has one, the car, like a villa by the sea, is only desirable and useful insofar as the masses don't have one. (Gorz, 1973)

Consequently, "The automobile is the paradoxical example of a luxury object that has been devalued by its own spread." Many anti-car intellectuals have echoed Gorz's insight with more detail but less wit. Whereas Adorno defined "luxury" in esthetic terms, Gorz perceived in 1960s Paris what Adorno should have understood in 1940s Los Angeles. It is logistically impossible for all to enjoy the privilege – or luxury, if you prefer – of the car-driver. Not only does the pollution become suffocating, Gorz observed, "when everyone claims the right to drive at the privileged speed of the bourgeoisie ... the average speed on the open road falls below the speed of a bicyclist" (Gorz, 1973). In Section 2, when we look at the adoption of the motor car in the world's major cities before 1900, we will see how and why the elite, bourgeois status of the car was solidified in a manner that could not be undone, despite the ardent support of both socialist and fascist politicians.

1.2 Post-Humanist Theory behind the Wheel: Donna Haraway, Judith Butler

> *You know the difference between humans and animals? Animals can't drive. To drive makes us human.* Nissan engineer Hiroshi Tamura, a cult figure for his design of the 370Z and GT-R models.
>
> (Scherr, 2024: 79)

In the twenty-first century, social and critical theory has shifted away from Marxism and psychoanalysis toward feminist, ethnic studies, and environmental methodologies. Gramsci and Adorno's writings are not read or taught so often. Post-humanism is one product of this shift. But post-humanist theory has also ignored or misunderstood cars. Case in point: some people treat their cars better than their pets, or even better than their human kin. Pets have been central to post-humanist theory, particularly Donna Haraway's work, so why are cars excluded? Psychologists in Germany found that test subjects were more successful in matching photographs of people to photos of the cars they drove than to photos of their pets (Alpers, 2006).

The post-humanist movement, in its early stages around 2000, was made up of two camps, and to some degree, it still is. First, a technophilic post-humanism initiated by Haraway's "Cyborg Manifesto," which, with the advent of artificial intelligence, has spawned even more hyperbolic and futuristic variants. Second, a biophilic post-humanism that emphasizes the consciousness and intelligence of nonhuman species and the degree to which humans are entangled or enmeshed in a multispecies biotic world. The post-humanity of the car draws upon both strains, despite the fact that car-drivers are rarely recognized as cyborg entities and that cars are detested by some of the biophilic scholars.

Donna Haraway has been a leader for both camps.[1] Her "Cyborg Manifesto," first published in 1985, helped give a name and a style to the first, while her later work continues to inspire the multispecies or biophilic version. The word coined by two astrophysics scholars in a 1960 paper, is short for "cybernetic organism." Haraway, like Bruno Latour (who, early in his career, wrote a book on a planned transit network for Paris), aimed to deconstruct the major binary oppositions in the human sciences: "the Great Divides of animal/human, nature/culture, organic/technical, and wild/domestic." Cars would presumably belong in the technical, not the organic. But Haraway's goal is revealed at the end of that sentence; she asserts that each of these divides "... flatten into mundane differences" (Haraway, 2008: 15). Cars, the mundane, unnoticed cyborgs, are not only machines; they also have animal, human, and organic aspects. Two pages earlier, Haraway makes a grand claim for the impact of her post-humanist theory. She reviews Freud's account of "three great historical wounds to the primary narcissism of the self-centered human subject." First, the Copernican wound, which removed Earth from the center of the known universe; then the Darwinian wound, "which put *Homo sapiens* firmly in the world of other critters"; and finally Freud's own wound, "an unconscious that undid the primacy of conscious processes, including the reason that comforted Man with his unique excellence." Haraway then announces her own "fourth wound, the informatic or cyborgian, which infolds organic and technological flesh and so melds that Great Divide as well" (11–12). This serves as a good genealogy of post-humanism, moving from cosmological to biological to psychological to technological. The notion of "technological flesh" appropriates Maurice Merleau-Ponty's concept of the "flesh of the world" for the technophilic or cyborg strain. In Haraway's view, one cannot easily draw a line between human and machine, organic and technical.

A few sociologists have applied Haraway's concept to cars and drivers, which seems obvious. Timothy Luke linked the cyborg to automobility in a 1996 paper, singling out the Porsche 911 as a commodified machinic possession – one he saw as more dehumanizing than post-human. Australian Deborah Lupton wrote: "When one is driving, one becomes a cyborg, a combination of human and machine ... This merging of boundaries between human bodies and subjectivities and car bodies – the production of the car/driver" (Lupton, 1999: 59).

---

[1] Haraway was aware of this conflict. At the start of *Where Species Meet*, she recalls a 2001 conference where she was assailed by Deep Ecologists: "If one loves organic nature, to express a love of technology makes one suspect. If one finds cyborgs to be promising sorts of monsters, then one is an unreliable ally in the fight against the destruction of all things organic" (10). A love of cars, which I fully confess, is not a love of technology, however, it is a love of human art and artifice.

Haraway came close to considering the car-driver in the cheeky introduction to *When Species Meet*, where she made a quip linking it to her earlier work: "I want my people, those collected by figures of moral relatedness, to go back to that old political button from the late 1980s, 'Cyborgs for earthly survival,' joined to my newer bumper sticker from *Bark* magazine, 'Dog is my co-pilot'" (2008, 16). Haraway evidently affixed that bumper sticker to her own car, in which she carried her dog. A long footnote about the "Darwin Fish" stickers suggests she is aware of the discourses of bumper stickers – symbols and catchphrases that respond to and rebut other stickers in ongoing arguments. Let's revise Haraway's work by adding "driver/car" to her list of Great Divides that ought to be melded and flattened. The driver/car, or car-driver, is also an "infolding of organic and technological flesh," a mundane cyborg. Haraway's car, along with the millions of other cars Americans depend upon, have become a plague that threatens Earth's health. Car-drivers fondly proclaim pride and identity in defense of their habit (or habitus) and resist change. The "Dog is my co-pilot" sticker riffs on a popular Christian bumper sticker, "God is my co-pilot," but it also has a more literal meaning, obvious when one sees a driver sharing their seat with their dog, whose head sticks out the window or sunroof. When I see canine co-pilots, I ponder the sanctity and the sanity of the pilots. I'm also reminded of the sticker when at the home and garden store where I annually purchase bags of "Bark and Steer" fertilizer.

Are animals and cars comparable in their relationships to humans? One's answer may depend on whether the car or animal has agency or consciousness and can be recognized as a sentient being. The gaze of the animal is a common conceit of post-humanist and animal studies scholars. Fewer humans would acknowledge the gaze of a car, but cars do have faces, as I will demonstrate in the next section. The "animal other" is a pet concept for many post-humanists and humanists, who decry the oppression of animals, advocate for the rights of animals, and seek to speak for or understand the consciousness of various animals. The rhetoric and law of animal rights often follow that of human rights and of advocacy on behalf of social groups who are minoritized, oppressed, or "othered." Social activists and theorists are much less likely to appeal on behalf of people who lack cars. Yet many people in the United States who lack cars or can't drive face severe restrictions on access to employment, health care, and other necessities. When money becomes available, many poor people will buy or fix a car to address a need that can improve their lives.

Reluctance to admit cars into the expanded circle of agential beings that post-humanist theory has proposed may arise because post-humanists see cars more as their self than as their other. They don't ascribe to a car independent agency or consciousness, as they do to pets or wild animals. A car, most assume, expresses the agency and identity of its driver. But can a car be a living body? Brenda Jo Bright, one of the best car scholars of the 1990s, in an article on Northern New Mexico lowriders, elaborates on her informant's comment that he has a "heart like a car." She adds that the blending of body parts and machine "suggests the ways in which the car is an embodiment, enhancing both bodily mobility and affectivity. In this vein, the car resembles the human body, and both are sites of cultural inscription" (Bright, 1998: 596). The car is humanoid in part because humans made cars in their own image. Consider the Renaissance origins of modern humanism, when artists from da Vinci to Milton rendered God and angels in human form and anthropomorphized continents, winds, cities, and abstract virtues. Cars are also creations of human ingenuity, and many lowriders are adorned with Catholic religious art.

Leading post-humanist theorists like Haraway rarely write about cars, but in interviews, they reveal something of their everyday lives and their cars. For a profile published in *The New Yorker,* the journalist visited Judith Butler in Berkeley, California:

> Butler apologized for the mess in their car, an old BMW ... a few books by the phenomenologist Maurice Merleau-Ponty, strewn around the back seat ... "My proprioceptive body" is how Butler refers to their car. "I'm surrounded by this clunky thing, and I feel protected," they explained. "I expand, I have this carapace." They laughed. "But it's, um, prosthetic." (Seghal, 2024)

Butler's apology and self-deprecating reference to "this clunky thing" suggest they are bashful about their fondness for the collectible BMW (which requires careful and costly maintenance). Butler's response to being outed as a car enthusiast is to theorize it in post-humanist or material feminist terminology and to pun on the letters c-a-r (as I also do). The term "prosthesis," also used by Haraway in her writings about the cyborg, refers to a device that has no function apart from the human body to which it is attached and is often crafted to fit a specific user. Tim Dant equates cyborg and prosthesis: "the term 'cyborg' properly refers to the feedback systems incorporated into the body that can be used to replace or enhance human body parts" and differentiates it from "The driver-car [which] is neither a thing nor a person; it is an assembled social being that takes on properties of both and cannot exist without both" (Dant, 2005: 74). The cyborg is both human and machine, whereas the car-driver is neither, yet combines aspects of each.

Cars are not prostheses designed for and employed by individual bodies; they are mass-produced for consumers. However, a car-driver does have proprioceptive affordances distinct from those of the human body, and can qualify as a cyborg, in Haraway's sense. But the car-driver need not be part of an individual body. In another social context, such as a car club for BMW owners, Butler and the "clunky thing" would have an identity distinct from her academic career. And one could imagine the BMW has a social identity of its own for some in the neighborhood who see Butler driving it but don't know her except as the driver of that car. Cars have faces, reputations, and styles. A person uses a prosthesis to restore, extend, or modify their senses, affordances, or abilities. A car's owner modifies it not to extend or restore their pre-existing identity but to create a separate, distinct automotive identity, which I would call a "caracter," not a carapace.

The post-humanist trend in theory and cultural studies has been strongest among feminist scholars in literature, philosophy, and anthropology. It has been less influential in sociology, even as the field promoted studies of automobility, which drew on post-humanist methods. John Urry and Mimi Sheller's paper "The City and the Car," as well as several subsequent publications by Urry and other co-authors, defined automobility to include cars and trucks, roads and parking lots, the entire "machinic complex" of related industries, and the ideology and habitus that have made automobility the "predominant global form of 'quasi-private' mobility" and "the single most important cause of environmental resource-use" (Sheller & Urry, 2000: 738–739). That paper also defined the car-driver very broadly: "a 'hybrid' assemblage, not simply of autonomous humans, but simultaneously of machines, roads, buildings, signs and entire cultures of mobility" (739). This definition of automobility is, in my view, too broad, too urban, too modernist, and too technophilic. Urry characterized the private car as "literally [Max] Weber's 'iron cage' of modernity, motorized, moving, and privatized," which has led to "a 'nasty, brutish, and short' world of millions of moving and crashing iron cages" (Urry, 2006: 20, 23). The cage metaphor ignores the ways car-drivers communicate on the road in a "civil society of automobility," a term that Urry and Sheller used but is better articulated by others, such as Jörg Beckmann (2001). Dant prefers the term "driver-car" rather than "car-driver" to emphasize this civility of the roadscape: "Driving, especially in traffic, depends on a mutual social cooperation that expresses an unspoken solidarity, a 'conscience collective' that is taken for granted and only noticed when a transgression occurs" (Dant, 2009: 257). Richard Randell, invoking Erving Goffman, calls it the *autoself*: "the product of routine, automobile public performances. The road then becomes the locus of production of the autoself; not the private, interior cabin of the automobile where human bodies and machines merge into a cyborg entity" (Randell, 2016: 4).

The emotive value of car faces, I will argue in the next section, proves that car-drivers are interacting in the most basic nonverbal ways, just as ambulatory humans do with their facial expressions, clothing, and grooming. In the more diverse roadscapes of developing countries, pedestrians, motorcycles, rickshaws, carts, and indeed animals interact face-to-face and through horns, gestures, and expressive movement. In these settings, "the boundary between road and surrounding land is somewhat blurred ... roadside spaces are not diminished by regulation but are sites for social interaction and enterprise, vastly different from the socially sterile, 'purified,' 'single purpose' verges in Western countries" (Edensor, 2004: 110). Even in the "purified" settings that resemble Urry's description, however, communication among car-drivers does occur.

1.3 "Cars Have Their Own Faces": Roadscape as Post-Human Environment

The face-to-face interaction of travelers in roadscapes implies an important aspect of both the car and the driver. Drivers and passengers inside modern cars are mostly concealed from the view of other road users, and for this reason, many treat the car as a private space (as Urry's papers asserted). But cars have faces, and recognition and interactions among car-drivers can be transacted by these faces. Car-drivers who are not car enthusiasts, and who do not quickly recognize the brands and model-years of other cars, interact using semi-conscious faculties that are hybrids of the driver's face and hands, which occasionally can make direct contact with other road users, and the car's forms of visual, aural, and haptic communication, which are more crude, but more evident at a distance.

Car designers and marketers have long known about car faces. For example, Peter Horbury, vice president for design at Geely Holding Group, the Chinese company that acquired Volvo in 2010, in an interview with Pulitzer Prize–winning *Wall Street Journal* car critic Dan Neil, said "The face is important because the face will tell everybody the character of the car" (Neil, 2012). Features that designers want to highlight in a new model: speed and agility, safety and security, rugged reliability, or intimidating size and strength, need to be expressed in the car's front or face. Psychologists and anthropologists have confirmed the designer's techniques with sophisticated measurements of human perception and cognition.

Sonja Windhager was a PhD student in anthropology at the University of Vienna in 2008 when she became the lead author of "Face to Face: The Perception of Automotive Designs" in the journal *Human Nature*. The study began with high-resolution 3D computer models of thirty-eight cars, representing twenty-six manufacturers, from the 2004 to 2006 model-years. Forty research subjects were shown images of the cars' fronts and asked to rate the cars based on social/emotional traits, including afraid, happy, surprised, agreeable, content, aroused, and disgusted, as well as demographics such as child-adult and male-female. The researchers reported: "people generally agreed in their ratings. Thus, there must be some kind of consistent information that is being perceived in car fronts. However, a few traits lacked such agreement (disgusted, extroverted, sad, neurotic, and conscientious)" (Windhager et al., 2008: 340). Setting aside these more subtle emotions, the researchers schematized the car faces using geometric morphometrics based on thirty-four landmarks, the points marking the location and outline of windshield, headlights, grille, lower air intake slots, rearview mirrors, and tires. These data enabled determination of the landmarks most diagnostic in classifying a car's face along thirteen of the social/emotional factors. Shape-trait partial least squares analysis then stretched the schematic image of a car front to maximize and minimize these factors, creating extreme versions of car design.

An illustration from the 2008 paper (Figure 1) shows that the friendly, agreeable, childlike, female car has a higher windshield and a narrower face, with headlights above the grille, resembling the face of an infant. In the car-face at the contrasting extreme, "Headlights become more angular in the direction of increasing 'power' . . . having the eyebrows drawn down, particularly at the inner ends. Thus, the association of hostility and arrogance is not surprising" (341). Subjects were also asked to rate how much they liked each car, and the morphometric analysis of their preferences closely resembled the hostile, male, arrogant, dominant car front on the right. The authors acknowledge how these principles may already be known to car designers: "With respect to practical applications, a tool for automobile designers to style cars according to a desired image could be derived" (343). Their findings will be unsurprising to feminists and help explain why prominent post-humanist scholars, many of whom are women, have avoided cars in their formulations of the cyborg, animal, and monster, figures of power, to which they claim women have affinity and affordance.

Windhager and co-authors considered a counterargument: test subjects may have recognized the brand identities of the car fronts and associated power, aggressiveness, or other traits shown in the right-hand schematic with the higher-prestige brands. For instance, "Cars of high 'power' also tend to be the more expensive, prestigious, high quality, of greater engine capacity" (342). For a follow-up study published in *Evolution and Human Behavior* in 2012, the team of six researchers added an Ethiopian colleague who collected data from subjects in that country, of whom just "11 of 89 participants reported having a driver's license and 6 claimed to own a car" (Windhager et al., 2012: 111). Even though the Ethiopians were presumably less influenced by car advertising

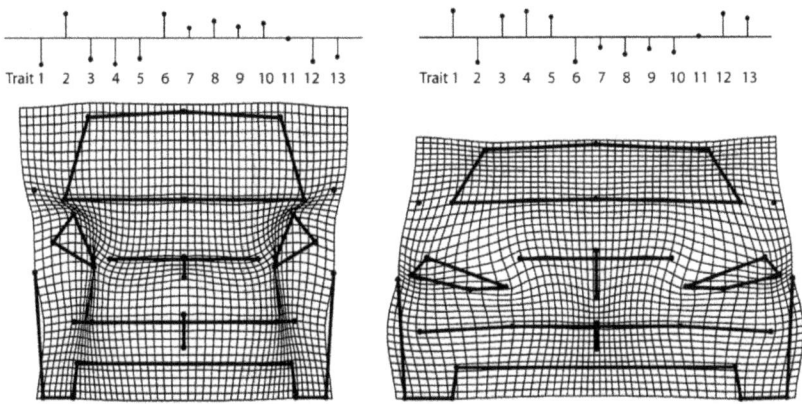

Figure 1 Shape change partial least squares analysis of car fronts, from Windhager et al.

Note: The two schematics represent maximum and minimum values of these thirteen anthropomorphic or emotional assessments: child-adult (1), male-female (2), friendly-hostile (3), submissive-dominant (4), angry (5), afraid (6), happy (7), surprised (8), open (9), agreeable (10), content (11), arrogant (12) and aroused (13).

than the Austrian subjects, they nonetheless agreed closely on these ratings, and new schematic drawings were very similar to Figure 1. One notable difference: "all cars were judged as 'arrogant' in Ethiopia" (118).

Windhager and co-authors collaborated on another paper in an anthropology journal, arguing for the modern evolutionary advantage of being able to quickly recognize cars' faces. This paper built upon earlier functional magnetic resonance imaging (fMRI) research showing that the fusiform face area in research subjects' brains was activated by images of car fronts as easily as by images of human faces (Gauthier et al., 2000). This propensity for seeing faces, for "interpreting the non-living as living and in human terms" the authors capture in the phrase "'better safe than sorry!' That is, we gain much from being right (e.g. identifying another human, predator, prey) in vague reality and lose little when accidentally treating a non-agent as an agent" (Windhager et al., 2010: 1075). This is an important public health issue: In many countries around the world, especially in Africa, being hit by a car or truck is one of the leading causes of death among children and people in their prime working years. Cars (some named for dangerous animals such as Jaguar, Cougar, Lynx, Bobcat, Stingray, Barracuda, or Cobra) have replaced wild animals as major threats to humans' life and limb. To be able to perceive an oncoming car within 100 milliseconds is an important survival skill. The faces of cars facilitate cognitive perception of them more quickly than our brains can recognize other things, say, a falling tree trunk or boulder, which might also pose a sudden life-or-death risk. The distinctions between non-agent and agent, nonliving and living, animal and human are not settled questions for post-humanists, as they were for the social scientists studying car faces. Much of the most influential post-humanist research, including biosemiotics, is about blurring these boundaries. For instance, Robin Wall Kimmerer's enormously popular work argues that stones can be alive (Goddard, 2002; Kimmerer, 2015: 61–66). Haraway, Anna Tsing, and others argue for the animacy of plants and the influence of multispecies assemblages. I ask post-humanist scholars to consider evidence that car-drivers are agents, and cars are, in some sense, alive.

The anthropologists' research relied on images of early 2000s cars and did not consider the history of car design, but I contend that headlights have been the eyes of cars' faces since they were invented. The first cars did not have lights installed, even if they were tested at night when roads were empty (see Maxim, 1936: 87–91). Until the 1930s, cars' lights were nearly always large, round brass or steel units attached to the bumper or chassis of the car; they were not incorporated into the fenders or grille. The 2010 paper, "Laying Eyes on Headlights: Eye Movements Suggest Facial Features in Cars," asked test subjects in eye-tracking experiments to compare the eyes, ears, mouth, and nose of human faces with car faces. Their eyes fixed most frequently upon the headlights, regardless of what they were asked to compare. This study confirmed the protocol of the geometric morphometrics we saw in Figure 1 and that eyes are always the most salient part of a face. They found that "if asked to compare the nose, the mean number of fixations was more than twice as high for the grille as for the other features, i.e., the air intake and the side-view mirrors. Similarly, numbers of fixations were more than doubled for the side-view mirrors and the ears when participants had to 'compare the ears'" (Windhager et al., 2010: 1078). Rearview mirrors and lower air intakes became common on cars much later than headlights, which further supports the evolutionary psychology of paying close attention to the headlights of vehicles rather than other parts of their faces.

Scholars in environmental humanities have dipped into evolutionary anthropology by using the concept of the *umwelt* to better understand how humans and nonhuman animals both construct cognitive models of their environments. The term was popularized by Jakob Johann von Uexküll in the early 1930s (when car fronts were very different) and has been used in a naturalistic way, for example, as a means to appreciate how ticks and other insects employ very different sensory information than humans and similar mammals do. Science journalist Carole Kaesuk Yoon expanded the use of umwelt to the modern urban environments most humans now share (Yoon, 2009: 280–282). She argued that children learn corporate logos and cartoon characters from media using the same capacity for assiduous observation through which children once learned about the plant and animal species they saw outdoors. This was true for me growing up in the 1970s. I often played outdoors, catching crawdads in the creek behind my neighborhood, and I enjoyed books about cougars and other big cats, but my skill for identifying species of bugs and plants was diverted to brands and models of cars. Yoon likewise asserts that the human cognitive genius for identifying and naming plants and animals has been detoured into consumer products. Even two-year-olds can identify many different brand logos, according to social science experiments, and so can animals like crows and bears. These animals often scavenge for human food by looking for packaging emblazoned with logos such as McDonald's or Safeway. Children also learn the faces or general physiognomy of cars and perceive that cars express emotions just as human and nonhuman faces do. Car designers are aware of this as well, as the interview by Dan Neil of Peter Horbury shows.

For children today, the idea that cars have faces may be semi-conscious common knowledge, but many will also think of the Disney movie franchise. The *Cars* filmmakers opted for full animism by putting expressive, blinking eyes in the windshields of the caracters. Disney/Pixar artists may have communicated with art college friends working in the car industry. They already knew that higher windshields make for childlike or submissive faces, as with Luigi and Mater. Peter Horbury said he agreed with the animators that the headlights are redundant, and the windshield is a portal, a mirror by which car-drivers gain conscious agency and affect, which may originate in a human driver or, as in the *Cars* films and some car-horror films, in a cinematic character. Like many Disney animated movies from decades earlier, *Cars* relied on ethnic, regional, and gender stereotypes that I will explore and critique below, as well as gender norms explicit in an early scene at a racetrack, where fans entering the men's restroom are pickup trucks and SUVs, and those waiting in line at the women's restroom are small sedans, coupes, and roadsters such as the Mazda Miata, also the model of the female groupies who dote on Lightning and other racing stars. The animated films showed millions of viewers the rich cultural symbolism of car design.

2 Cars and the Anthropocene

2.1 "The Earth Is Inhabited by Strange Creatures Called Cars ... "

> A biologist from a pedestrian planet, peering at some stretch of North America from a height of five hundred feet, will conclude that its dominant species is a shiny

lozenge-shaped reptilian creature that alternately basks in the sun and sprints at great speed. It is host, he will note, to small endosymbiotic organisms which at intervals emerge, move about slowly, then re-enter the host. Further observation reveals why the host puts up with these seeming parasites. They are devoted to the care and feeding of the host. They suck energy-rich organic compounds from the bowels of the planet and feed them to the host, something it is unable to do for itself. At times they even fight other colonies of their own species for access to the host food. They make over ecosystems to meet the host's needs, replacing vast forests and grasslands with flat surfaces on which the host can bask or sprint more easily, and building hives or dens in which the host can take shelter from the elements. What they get in return is as yet unclear. Indeed, it seems possible the two organisms are forms of the same species, the lozenge being a sort of queen and the smaller creature a worker.

(Eisenberg, 1998: 56)

When I used to accompany my daughter to her school bus I often made up stories to amuse her as we walked. One was a description of the earth and its inhabitants as told by an alien examining us from a spaceship above London. This alien had observed that the earth is inhabited by strange creatures called cars, mainly with four wheels although some are great beasts with twelve wheels and some little creatures with only two. These creatures are served by a host of slaves who walk on legs and spend their whole lives serving them. The slaves constantly ensure that the cars are fed their liquid foods whenever they are thirsty and are cured if they have accidents: but the slaves also help in the reproduction and disposal of cars. The slaves are deposited in boxes set up almost everywhere a car wants to go and are always ready to be taken away as soon as the car makes up its mind to go somewhere else. Cars were never seen to go anywhere without at least one slave. The slaves build and maintain long and complex networks of clear space so that cars have little trouble travelling from place to place. Indeed, the earth's creatures seem constantly pampered by their fawning army of slaves.

(Miller, 2001: 1)

Two versions of this sci-fi parable offer further proof that the car-driver is a cyborg, or a multi-species organism, and that its prevalence constitutes a distinct epoch in the biological and social history of the planet. Eisenberg calls it "a reptilian creature," a metaphor that matches the alternating frantic movement and eerie idleness of cars and trucks in traffic, as well as the radiant heat of paved "flat surfaces on which the host can bask or sprint more easily." The symbiosis of the car as host to human parasites matches the mutual dependence of the two creatures. Symbiosis is also an ecological relation embraced by post-humanist theories, including those of Haraway and Tsing, although Eisenberg never mentions post-humanism in his book. Miller, who used the term "Humanity of the Car" before I adopted it as the title for a 2020 article, offers instead a master/slave dialectic, although his text never mentions Hegel or the philosophical tradition spawned by the famous passage in *Phenomenology of Spirit*.

A master/slave or lord/bondsman (*Herr/Knecht*) relationship between car and driver doesn't match post-humanist theory as closely as the host/parasite, but it is no less prophetic. Humans invented cars first as a toy suitable only for lords and the haute bourgeoisie, but soon after, they produced many more cars and promoted them as vehicles of independent mobility, also known as freedom. So long as cars were considered machines with no self-consciousness, the insidious master/slave dialectic could not begin. But "replacing vast forests and grasslands" with "long and complex networks of clear space" destroyed the original habitat and sustenance of horses and pedestrian "slaves," who quickly became dependent upon cars. Perhaps because Miller is British, he imagines the slaves "deposited in boxes" by the cars, whereas an American accustomed to attached garages might have written that cars are the lords of their manors, in which the servants provide cars with shelter as well as feeding. In the eyes of anti-car activists, a life-or-death struggle would be the next stage in the tale. More relevant for our purposes, however, is Hegel's concept of mutual recognition and self-consciousness, which is necessary to resolve the dialectic.

The story of automobility, as viewed by extraterrestrials, is instructive because it explains the role not only of mobility but also of domesticity in the car/driver relationship. Most private cars sit empty for at least 90 percent of their working lives, inside or nearby their owner's dwellings, and owners are content to absorb the costs of this idleness, notably the depreciation and insurance. Efforts to displace private cars in urban areas with short-term car-rental services like ZipCar or shared autonomous vehicles such as Waymo have barely earned enough customers to stay in business. I propose to examine the problem of car-dependence not as economic, geographic, or logistical, but as psychological. Only if drivers (and passengers) recognize how cars have become active agents in their lives – how their alter ego as a car-driver is a pleasure and/or a curse – can car-dependence be acknowledged, and programs for addiction recovery be designed. In this scenario, post-humanist theorists offer some limited insight. "Her techno-monsters contain enthralling promises of possible re-embodiments," writes Rosi Braidotti of Donna Haraway, "the cyborg, the monster, the animal – the classical 'other than' the human – are thus emancipated from the category of pejorative difference and shown in a more positive light" (Braidotti, 2002: 243). Braidotti does discuss cars briefly in a chapter titled "Meta(l)morphoses: the Becoming Machine," but the topic there is J. G. Ballard's novel *Crash*, the death of Princess Diana, and the film *Thelma and Louise*. The car as cyborg, according to Braidotti, occurs when a crash victim bears "visible traces of their intercourse with the technological other" (236). Because Braidotti and Haraway see cyborgs as high-tech and apocalyptic, as sci-fi sensations, whereas driving a car is mundane, they fail to recognize the car-driver as a post-human agent. Moreover, the cyborg, monster, and animal are "other" (even if that is a difference raised only to be flattened, to use Haraway's phrase), whereas the car, as we saw in the previous section, is an expression of its driver's self or a being potentially equal to the self, given a condition of true self-consciousness.

I have argued that the car-driver is a life form, a hybrid species-being that has evolved in the modern era since 1900. I don't wish to add "Carocene" to the already lengthy and comical list of alternative names for the Anthropocene; I simply want to point out how, if one looks at Earth's landscapes from high above, as the aliens do, the prominence of paved roads, parking lots, garages, and services for cars and trucks constitutes the most noticeable and widespread change humans have made to Earth. Even the ubiquitous cornfields of the American Midwest are part of the infrastructure of automobility. More than 60 percent of the corn growing each summer in Iowa, where I grew up, is refined into ethanol to fuel cars and trucks. Thousands of years in the future, the metal, plastic, glass, and rubber detritus of nearly two billion cars will be evidence of what life on Earth was like in our time.

The tale of aliens visiting Earth and identifying cars as the dominant life form might be more plausible in a version where the aliens arrive in a distant future after the car-driver is extinct, and they interpret the detritus and "cartifacts" to determine the largest and most numerous species. That would be a geological, stratigraphic narrative suitable to the common definition of the Anthropocene. The story was not created in that form because it is, after all, an apocalyptic fantasy, and like others in the apocalyptic genre, it is anthropocentric and solipsistic. Its overt meaning, at least in Daniel Miller's version, is that humans have become enslaved by cars – a version of the common sci-fi premise of aliens invading Earth and dominating humans. But its covert meaning elevates the status of the car-driver hybrid into Earth's dominant life form, more important and powerful than the ambulatory human. Car and human resolved their master/slave dialectic with a merger; humans need cars to define and enable their identity. Like the fantasy of the autonomous vehicle, which engaged both Detroit and Silicon Valley corporations from about 2014 to 2022, the tale describes an apotheosis of the car – an automobility that has become a theology for the modern secular age. Having made the car in our own image, humans have now made the car-driver the prime mover in our daily routines.

This folkloric detour helps explain why the Anthropocene should be defined as the epoch during which Earth's dominant life form became the automobile, together with its parasitic owner/driver, joined as car-driver. Many scholars of the Anthropocene, notes Andreas Malm, have "suggested that James Watt's invention of the steam-engine inaugurated the new epoch, and the chronology stuck: in the burgeoning literature on the Anthropocene, the steam-engine is often referred to as the one artifact that unlocked the potentials of fossil energy and thereby catapulted the human species to full-spectrum dominance" (Malm & Hornborg, 2014: 63). Literary scholars working in a new materialist paradigm, such as Imre Szeman and Patricia Yaeger, have proposed a study of the Anthropocene focused on the various heat engines and the fuel sources that powered them: whale oil for lamps, then coal as the fuel for steam capitalism, followed by petroleum for internal combustion engines.

It may seem reasonable to use the energy-based method to study cars and automobility as well. The current effort to decarbonize transportation by replacing internal combustion engines with battery electric motors is consistent with this logic. The weakness of the method is the implied technological determinism linking motors and fuels. Coal was not the only fuel for steam engines. Railroad locomotives and steamships in the nineteenth century were sometimes powered with wood, and from 1899 to 1924, when US steam car manufacturers Locomobile (a name combining "locomotive" and "automobile") and its successor, the Stanley Motor Carriage Company, challenged the incipient dominance of internal combustion cars (internal referring to the contrast with steam boilers heated externally), the steam engines burned kerosene or naphtha, not coal. Consequently, one should not expect a change in the fuel that powers cars to alleviate the ills they cause. Hydrogen should not be labeled "clean" or "green" any more than horses. In place of the conventional notion that the industrial revolution, powered by coal-burning steam engines, began the Anthropocene in the early nineteenth century, which then accelerated with the capitalist exploitation of petroleum, natural gas, and uranium, I suggest a study of the infrastructure of automobility – of the cars and roads that have reshaped Earth and have changed human behavior more profoundly than the fuels and engines that remain invisible and poorly understood by the humans who use them. Instead of a new materialist analysis, I offer a humanist, functionalist approach to the Anthropocene that examines the invention and popularization of cars as linked to and built upon the forms of transportation they superseded: horses and the carriages they pulled, as well as the roads on which both competed for rights-of-way.

2.2 The Horseless Carriage Age: Anthropocene as the Epoch of Cars

A brief history of how cars began to change life in the United States in the late nineteenth century will illuminate and support the case for the humanity of the car, and counter methodologies that fetishize or hypostatize the car as a machine, an error as common among car critics as among car boosters. Car defenders have repeatedly promised that new inventions will alleviate the ills of the machine, or the externalities of automobility, as economists phrase it: pollution, congestion, and resource depletion. Car critics have often failed to see how alternatives or resistance to cars should focus not simply on the vehicles (car, bicycle, train) but on the routes vehicles use (road, path, rail) and that structure urban spaces. One should understand the car and the car-driver as creations, collectively, of the industrial system that manufactured vehicles, of the road system that was built for vehicles to travel on, and of the fuels they consumed. Roads, not only cars, are evidence that automobility initiated the Anthropocene. Looking back at the early years of powered transportation in America, from the 1880s to the success of the Model T in the early 1910s, we will see how cars displaced carriages, wagons, and bicycles, and how today's battles between bikes and cars for control of the roadscape arose out of a very different relationship a century earlier.

I use the word "car" because it is an old word that links horse-drawn wagons, chariots, or carriages to motor cars. Roger Bacon, in a thirteenth-century treatise, wrote of "the battle-cars of the ancients, with their formidable wheels, armed with scythes and sickles" (Pettifer & Turner, 1984: 36). By contrast, "automobile" is a modern loan word that became popular in English in the 1890s when the French led the world in motor car technology. I see continuities between carriages and cars, and the term "horseless carriage," first used in 1895, reveals continuity between horsecars, carriages, and early motor cars. This section builds upon research by historian Clay McShane in *Down the Asphalt Path: The Automobile and the American City.*

When colonial American cities were platted, streets were public spaces where children could play, and everyone could work, socialize, do housekeeping, and prepare food. Only a few wagons and carts drawn by horses, mules, or oxen traveled on these streets. Very few carriages (animal-drawn vehicles for human passengers, not cargo) existed in America until the 1810s. Trade commodities and cargo traveled in ships at sea, and in sailboats, barges, and canoes on rivers and canals. In the early 1800s, in the New York–Philadelphia area, governments began to authorize privately owned "graded paved turnpikes [which] lowered transportation costs by up to 50 percent, creating traffic that the steam railroads would later take over." City-dwellers took measures to preserve the safety of their streets as traffic increased. Municipal ordinances "required carters and teamsters to walk alongside their horses, rather than drive them in congested areas of cities" (McShane, 1994: 4–5). These teams and carts were slow and costly, "an 1875 study of freight facilities in New York points out that it cost $7.50 a ton to ship freight all the way from New York to Chicago, but that local delivery costs added $5.00 a ton" (44–45).

The advent of steam-powered transport in the early nineteenth century was not the epochal shift it may appear to be in hindsight, and I believe the steam-engine should not be used to mark the start of the Anthropocene. Paddle-wheel ships and early railroad locomotives were often fueled by wood, not by coal, and both forms of powered transport increased the dependence on horses and oxen, wagons, and hackneys, which were essential for the last mile (or more) of travel for the cargoes and passengers that steamships and trains carried. As steam-powered trade and travel grew, so did horse populations, and most of the additional animals were urban residents, not visitors from the countryside. In 1900, the US Census enumerated horses for the first time: New York City had over 130,000, Chicago counted 74,000 horses and mules, Philadelphia 51,000, and St. Louis 32,000 (McShane, 1994: 43–44). Teamsters, grooms, and stable hands had to support these growing herds in the middle of dense cities. The largest employers of horses in most cities were rail and streetcar companies. The consequences for cities were dire: "In the 1880s, New York City was removing 15,000 dead horses from its streets each year" (Pettifer & Turner, 1984: 51).

Surging horse populations increased congestion, noise, and collisions, as well as pollution and public health problems. Horse manure sometimes formed a layer covering roads inches deep. A horse produces more than 20 lbs. of manure each day, and a key factor motivating the use of asphalt to pave roads, which began in the US cities in the early 1870s, was that it created a smooth, impermeable surface from which manure could be more easily cleaned than from wood, granite blocks, or cobblestones. Concrete was also smooth, but the formula used at the time fractured too easily under the impact of horseshoes. Depending on local resources, cobblestones in a matrix of sand or mud, blocks of granite or another dense type of stone, or wooden blocks or planks were used to pave streets. Around 1816, Scottish engineer John Loudon McAdam developed a method of laying a thick foundation of 7.5 cm diameter stones and a surface of 2 cm stones, which then fractured under the impact of carriage wheels to create a semiimpermeable surface that came to be called macadam. This version of early gravel roads became common for turnpikes and was also the most economical option for streets, although it could erode in rainstorms and break apart under the impact of heavy, faster vehicles such as early steam-powered cars. Asphalt pavement was introduced in New York and Washington in the 1870s. Initially derived from bitumen imported from Pitch Lake, Trinidad, and other tar pits, Belgian chemist Edward de Smedt subsequently developed methods for combining petroleum with solid bitumen, which reduced the cost of asphalt paving.

Financing new paving projects was a challenge; it was costly because of the quantity of material required, the high labor costs typical in the United States in the nineteenth century, and the fees exacted by patentees such as Samuel Nicholson, who invented a system of wooden blocks milled to fit tightly together. Local governments most often charged street abutters for paving, but this was difficult because abutters often did not want the street in front of their property paved, or they would agree to pay only for the cheapest form of pavement. Real estate developers as early as 1800 agreed to pave streets (with cobblestone or occasionally wood or granite blocks) in exchange for title to some or all of the property adjoining the new street, or they might pave roads in return for the annexation of an entire new development by a municipality.

Nonetheless, many urban residents, some of them also abutters, resisted or protested the paving of streets fronting or near their homes and businesses. They knew that the changes that came with paved roads would deprive them of their use of public road space and expose them to risks of collisions, as well as to noise and pollution. One cause of suburbanization or urban sprawl in the nineteenth-century United States was the construction of new housing served by transport infrastructure that enabled residents to commute to work – such as omnibuses, horsecars, and later electric trolleys. This development could more easily be achieved if streets were built and paved before or at the same time as adjoining lots were sold and homes built. This approach avoided disputes over routes for streetcar rails, as well as the need to get abutters to pay individual allotments for paving (J. A. Miller, 1941: 22). The word "commuter" was derived from the discounts on horsecar or omnibus fares offered to those who rode them frequently. The fares were "commuted" or reduced. These discounts, as well as the common practice of charging a flat fare – often 5 cents – for a ride of any distance, amounted to a form of subsidy paid by city-dwellers for the benefit of suburbanites. This practice continues in cities where the subway and/or bus system charges a flat fare per ride.

In histories of the United States, railroads often play a mythical, Promethean role. But "railroad" in the mid-1800s did not only refer strictly to steam-powered trains, it also applied to horsecars, especially following the 1852 invention by Alphonse Loubat of grooved iron rails installed flush with the street surface so they did not hinder other vehicles. "A horse could pull a vehicle at 30% higher speed on rails than on the rough pavements on the time, and haul twice as many passengers" (McShane, 1994: 14). Railroad development thus proceeded in two types: steam locomotive-powered rail lines, which carried both freight and passengers and served intercity routes as well as some commuters on rights-of-way that were separate from streets; and horsecars on rails and pavements that could be shared by other users. Horse propulsion still held key advantages for urban travel into the 1880s.

While cities and commuters welcomed early rail travel, they were wary of steam-powered streetcars because of frequent explosions. Americans had learned to fear large high-pressure steam boilers due to a series of deadly explosions involving locomotive and steamboat engines in the 1820s and 1830s. Steam-powered versions of the horsecar proved unpopular due to their smoke, noise, and risk of explosion, which led some to build cars that tried to hide their engines: "By

1835, American railroads had switched to steam power, but the largest cities prohibited them from using steam on downtown streets" (McShane, 1994: 12). The horsecar franchises granted by cities to streetcar entrepreneurs often prohibited switching from horses to steam engines or sharing tracks with steam-powered vehicles. These entrepreneurs sometimes paid to pave the streets as well as to install rails, and other wagons or carriages enjoyed having a paved wheel track and drove on or next to the rails. The franchisees still enjoyed better protection from competition than did hacks or omnibus companies. Our modern word "bus" comes from omnibus, a large horse-drawn coach in an urban setting, usually with defined routes, schedules, and fares. Transit pioneer George Shillibeer adopted the word from a Frenchman who developed such a service in Nantes in 1826 (J. A. Miller, 1941: 4).

Horses in American cities in the late nineteenth century lived hard, brief lives in squalid, crowded stables. Their working life was about four years, at 4–6 hours per day, and "an early report of the American Street Railway Association states that about forty percent of the entire investment of the average company was in horses and stables" (J. A. Miller, 1941: 27–28). A shift in opinion toward steam-powered transport occurred after the epizootic of 1872, an influenza affecting horses that struck the urban Northeast. Although mortality was only about 1%, so many horses were sickened that there were not enough healthy horses to remove dead ones from the streets, and transit and delivery services were severely restricted. Reports on the epizootic in the *New York Times* measured its severity, as well as the enormous numbers of horses in Manhattan employed by the railroad companies and residing at "the car stables." "Taking, as an instance, the block between Broadway and Seventh-avenue and Thirty-eighth and Thirty-ninth streets, which includes eight livery and boarding sables and 344 horses; of the latter, 216 are suffering so severely as to be incapable of work" (Oct. 25, 1872). Two weeks later, a devastating fire in Boston destroyed 776 buildings in the central business district, as firefighters were forced to tow their engines to the scene without assistance from their draft horses. Many attributed this devastating loss to the equine epizootic. If Donna Haraway and Rosi Braidotti had lived a century earlier, they would likely have been active in efforts to end the brutal mistreatment of horses.

Because exclusive luxury transportation was also horse-powered, horses and carriages still connoted nobility and style, even as public horsecars proliferated, pulled by beleaguered nags. City planners went to great effort to provide venues for wealthy horsemen to show off their horses and carriages. The 1860s and 1870s saw the construction of large parks designed by Frederick Law Olmsted and Calvert Vaux in New York City, Brooklyn, Boston, Buffalo, and Rochester (and later the Olmsted firm designed many more in cities farther west). Manhattan's

Central Park banned omnibuses and street railways from the park drives, and soon after, the firm was hired to design Prospect Park in Brooklyn. On the basis of that work, they published *Observations on the Progress of Improvements in Street Plans, With Special Reference to the Park-way Proposed to Be Laid Out in Brooklyn*. The pamphlet's pompous tone addresses wealthy citizens, who:

> ... have multifarious styles of vehicles in each of which a large number of different hands has been ingeniously directed to provide in all their several parts for the comfort, pleasure, and health with which they may be used. For the sake of elegance, as well as comfort and ease of draft, they are made extremely light and are supplied with pliant springs. They are consequently quite unfit to be used in streets adapted to the heavy wagons employed in commercial traffic, and can only be fully enjoyed in roads expressly prepared for them. In parks such roads are provided ... (Olmsted & Vaux, 1868: 20)

The new parkways would be prohibited to horsecars, omnibuses, wagons, hacks, and any vehicles apart from private carriages – a policy justified by the supposed health benefits and the increased value of the abutting real estate. By the 1890s, electric trolleys had become the preferred transit vehicle, motivating real estate development, but even so, the Charles River Speedway in Boston and the Harlem River Speedway in New York were constructed in the 1890s explicitly for horse-drawn carriages, as well as bicycles, and soon after, the earliest motor cars. "Strong class tensions accompanied the nineteenth-century increase in riding and driving. The carriage set had used deceptive politics to get their drives, a sign of unpopularity" (McShane, 1994: 46). The Olmsted firm's parkways in Buffalo, Boston, and St. Louis are now admired by many urban planners, who often deplore decisions made in the 1960s and 70s to transform some of the routes into expressways. Here we see the basic premise of André Gorz confirmed. The motor car was from the start a luxury product for elites, a privilege that negates itself if the masses are afforded access (as on an expressway). Roads designed for high-speed travel, prior to the invention of the motor car, set a pattern that has continued to favor wealthy car owners over poorer citizens. The early motorcar was for: "the dangerous antics of rich and foolish persons who treated the important new technology as another sporting pastime to fill their idle hours" (Pettifer & Thomas, 1984: 49).

These patterns of road building and regulation also guided the use of the bicycle, a transport innovation eagerly adopted in the 1880s by affluent males as a recreational toy. Riders flocked to the parkways of major cities to show off their machines, as well as their speed and sportsmanship – a virtue that carried strong classist values of amateurism. Roughly ten years later, driving cars likewise became a faddish sporting leisure activity for urban upper-class men, and some women. Both bicycles and cars were individualized mechanical modes of transport and display, which set their users apart from the masses, who walked or traveled by horse-drawn omnibus or cart, by steam railroad, ferry, or electric trolley. Bicyclists lobbied for paved streets and parkways, as Olmsted and other carriage owners had ten to twenty years before, because without smooth surfaces, many cyclists found their new machines were uncomfortable "boneshakers" best suited for use indoors, in dance halls and velodromes. The popularity of cars, like bicycles, grew as more road surfaces suitable for their use were constructed – a process that faced financial, legal, and social challenges because other road users and abutters often saw their interests as antithetical to those of car-drivers and bicyclists. "Turn of the century auto advocates applied the analogy of pro-bicycle decisions when they lobbied against urban attempts to ban the auto" (McShane, 1994: 118).

Many engineering and manufacturing techniques developed for the bicycle in the 1880s were subsequently used in cars. Bicycle historian Pryor Dodge lists: "lightweight steel tubing, wire spokes, chain and shaft drives, drop forging, adjustable ball bearings and roller bearings, the free-wheel clutch, differential and variable gears, single tube pneumatic tires, reliable brakes, acetylene lamps and dynamos for electric lights" (Dodge, 1996: 152). The failed efforts to develop successful steam and battery-electric-powered cars before 1890 (and there were many more inventors, companies, and models than most realize, given that this history has most often been written to explain the dominance of the internal combustion car) can, in part, be explained by the fact that bicycle technologies were not yet available to them.

Automobile pioneer Hiram Percy Maxim wrote in a memoir that the role of the bicycle was fundamental in creating a potential market for cars:

> The reason why we did not build mechanical road vehicles before this [1870] was because the bicycle had not yet come in numbers and had not directed men's minds to the possibilities of independent, long-distance travel over the ordinary highway. We thought the railroad was good enough. The bicycle created a new demand which it was beyond the ability of the railroad to supply. Then it came about that the bicycle could not satisfy the demand that it created. (Maxim, 1936: 4–5).

In the 1890s, many entrepreneurs and engineers trying to build gasoline, steam, or electric-powered cars began with bicycles (or with tri- or quadra-cycles, which were often marketed for women or for a woman and her beau to ride in tandem). Whereas carriages and wagons had heavy wooden components built to endure rough roads, including wheels with iron rims, bicycles had light steel frames and wheels with bearings and pneumatic tires. Such a platform could be powered by a small gasoline motor, which was much easier for these inventors to build, refine, and test. Maxim began his memoir with a sentimental story, stating that he first dreamt of building a car while riding his bicycle one night in 1892 from Salem, Massachusetts, where he was courting a young woman, to his home in Lynn. On a later visit to Salem:

> I happened upon a second-hand Columbia tricycle ... This machine fascinated me. It would not fall over. It was large and provided what seemed to me ample room for an engine. And, what was immensely appealing, there was that extra seat which someday might perhaps be occupied by a certain somebody. (Maxim, 1936: 9)

Maxim purchased a used tricycle for $30.

In the twenty-first century, bicyclists in many cities have advocated for more and safer bike lanes and bike parking. If more people use bicycles instead of cars for their daily commutes and routines, cities will benefit from reduced pollution and congestion, but road designs and car-drivers' attitudes are often unwelcoming to cyclists. With this moral imperative in mind, the tone of bicycle boosters is often adversarial, as seen in the title of the trenchant documentary *Bikes vs. Cars*. Cycling advocates reflect an avant-garde in the process of Carbolization described in Section 4; some in car-dependent cities see what they have lost and wish to reverse the policies that privileged cars and highways. These cycling advocates might be surprised to learn that, in late nineteenth-century America, the popularity of the bicycle closely preceded that of the car, and the two new machines followed a common path of technological development and social adoption.

Both bicycles and horse-drawn carriages were important models for motorized wheeled transport, and both were predecessors of the car and of automobility. This is true in technological, legal, and political spheres, as well as in philosophical humanism. Zach Furness explains how "a popular metaphor for the cyclist was the centaur – a half-man, half-horse creature from Greek mythology" (Furness, 2010: 23–25). Donna Haraway, who helped popularize the term, referred to "my cyborg myth" but did not develop the links to ancient mythical creatures as Furness does (Haraway, 1985: 72). Haraway's goal was to bury or overturn Edenic myths; "I'd rather be a cyborg than a goddess" is the manifesto's last sentence (108). I prefer to find continuities between ancient mythology and futuristic technology because today the mythological imagination, and even the spiritual faith, of many people is invested in technology (e.g., AI, space travel, medical and dietary tools for longevity) and in heroes such as Elon Musk, Steve Jobs, or Stephen Hawking, who have replaced saints or other traditional religious pantheons. I also see the horseless carriage and the bicycle centaur as useful ways to defamiliarize and mythologize the origins of the car-driver hybrid.

Early car entrepreneurs exploited bicycle technologies for their engineering, but for marketing, they more often invoked the horse-drawn carriage's social status. As early car designers sought to build vehicles to seat four or more, command higher prices, and handle the rough and muddy roads of the time, they followed the model of the wagon or carriage, not the bicycle. In these 1890s models, such as the curved-dash Oldsmobile runabout, the bestselling American-made car of the pre-Model T era, the engine was usually installed under the seats. The dashboard, a common feature of carriages, protecting the driver and passengers from mud and manure coming from horses' hooves and rear-ends, was carried over into the car and now contains the controls, gauges, and infotainment of the modern car. Evidence of links between the car, the car/driver, and the horses and carriages of more than a century ago is found in English etymology. Internal combustion (and electric) motors are still measured by "horsepower," long after the metaphor's relevance has become obscure, since very few drivers ride or work with horses.

However successfully the cost and prestige of carriage designs were signified in cars, the beauty of the horse itself was missing. Not until the motor was moved out from under the seats and placed in front of the dashboard did the "horseless carriage" of the 1890s transform into the familiar cars of the twentieth century. Placing the engine in the front gave a vehicle greater symmetry, and even today manufacturers design long, high hoods to connote power and speed, even if the engine does not need the space. Patrick Keiller interprets this shift in gender terms, calls front-engine, rear-drive cars "phallic" and describes rear-engine, air-cooled, or front-engine, front-drive designs as a neglected feminine style, exemplified in the mid twentieth century by Tatra and Panhard cars (Keiller, 2002).

Because early steam and internal-combustion-powered cars, with their noisy, smelly engines, often frightened horses (a problem Hiram Percy Maxim knew well), Uriah Smith of Battle Creek, Michigan, filed a US patent application in 1899 for "a forwardly-projecting figure of a horse's head, the neck portion of the figure being curved on lines merging into the outline of the contiguous portion of the [vehicle] body" (Smith, 1899). Five years later another inventor, Henry Hayes of Denver, Colorado patented "a figure of an animal, preferably a horse of approximately life-size, with means for attaching it to the front of a motor-vehicle in such manner that it may be propelled by the vehicle and present the appearance of a horse drawing the vehicle" (Figure 2; Hayes, 1904). Neither invention was successfully commercialized, and horses either learned to tolerate the cars around them, or they were forced off the roads. Nonetheless, these inventions suggest how, if a person riding a bicycle was a centaur, a human/horse hybrid, early cars were a horse/carriage hybrid.

Figure 2 Henry Hayes, Patent Application for Model Horse Vehicle Front, 1904

To a majority of urban and rural residents in the United States during the early 1900s, who could not afford or did not wish to buy cars, the horse and carriage were the desirable products with which cars competed or were compared. Many established carriage manufacturers diversified into cars, such as Rauch & Lang of Cleveland, Ohio. A 1912 advertisement for their electric car models boasted

Figure 3 Advertisement for Rauch and Lang Carriage Company, 1912, in *The Literary Digest*

how the firm "began making coaches, carriages, and broughams for well-to-do families" in 1853 (Figure 3). Electric cars resembled carriages because their batteries were smaller than most gasoline engines, and a few carmakers still offered "motor buggies" with engines under the seats. The social prestige of carriages, and their association with European aristocrats, continued in US car marketing long after. Words for styles of carriages, such as Berline, Brougham, Landau, Sedan, and Station Wagon, contributed design motifs and names for cars and continued to do so into the late twentieth century. Electric cars nearly disappeared from the roads until the twenty-first century, when they re-emerged as luxury status symbols.

3 Cars, Futurism, and Nostalgia

Around 1900, a car was an expensive toy for the rich, designed and marketed to imitate, and then displace, the horse-drawn carriages, which even fewer could afford. In the 1910s, led by the Model T Ford, cars spread to rural residents of the United States and to the middle classes. As Henry Ford's publicist Samuel Crowther described it: "If what has been thought to be a luxury product can be manufactured in quantities at a low price, then it may become a commodity and a necessity – that is what happened with automobiles" (Ford, 1926: 155). The car, as a force of modernity, gradually changed roadscapes from chaotic, lively settings for many species and many types of vehicles into an expressway monoculture. A century later, in the 2010s, futurists, entrepreneurs, and policymakers proclaimed another major change – autonomous vehicles (AVs), also known as self-driving cars, were coming soon and would also be ubiquitous, because the supposed advantages of AVs could be realized only if they operated in concert, away from human drivers and pedestrians. The fever of AV hype burned hot as tech giants Google and Apple, rideshare platform Uber, as well as carmakers Ford, GM, Tesla, and others, each invested billions of dollars in efforts to develop self-driving cars and to find profitable schemes to commercialize them as a product or a service. The bubble has gradually deflated, punctured by the inherent complexity of navigating roadscapes and by embarrassing crashes, including the death of bicyclist Elaine Herzberg, who was hit and killed on March 18, 2018, by a self-driving Uber. To tragedy was added farce in the misadventures of driverless taxis offered by GM's Cruise unit in San Francisco, which failed to yield to emergency vehicles and, in one humorous incident in April 2023, drove into freshly poured concrete.

The self-driving car is an ambitious, futuristic invention, and it does hold the potential to disrupt automobility and automakers' business models, but it is hardly a new idea. Engineers, entrepreneurs, and investors promoting AV hype may not know that self-driving cars have been promised since the 1930s. I argue that the futurist fantasies of the 2010s were built from pieces of nostalgia from the halcyon days of the Detroit 3 in the 1940s and 1950s.

3.1 Futurama and Autonorama

At the New York World's Fair in 1939–40, GM built an exhibit called Futurama. Fairgoers sat in seats on a conveyor belt, listening to a synchronized narrative as they looked down at a huge diorama covering nearly an acre of space in a giant exhibit hall – a model of a typical American landscape in 1960. Hundreds of model cars moving on the superhighways in Futurama were described as being guided by automatic controls that enabled them to travel at high speeds with no risk of collisions (Figure 4). The engineering techniques used to try to achieve the goal of self-driving cars have changed greatly in eighty-five years, as the same promise, or fantasy, has been recycled several times. Peter Norton, in his 2021 book *Autonorama: The Illusory Promise of High-Tech Driving*, identifies three subsequent phases of Futurama, in which US carmakers claimed to be developing self-driving cars that would eliminate the problems of congestion, crashes, and resource scarcity. The fourth phase was announced by GM at an exposition in China in 2010, and we will return to it in Section 4.

While we wait for self-driving cars to find practical widespread use, we should reflect on how the concept creates tension in the car-driver hybrid.

Figure 4 Control bridge in Futurama motorway model, from *Magic Motorways* (1940)

Self-driving features that reach level 2 or 3 automation on SAE International's 1-to-5 scale, such as Nissan's ProPilot Assist, Audi's Traffic Jam Pilot, Cadillac's Super Cruise, and Tesla's Autopilot, can control vehicles on highways and wide streets with clear lane markers. Unfortunately, some car owners expect more capable computers than actually exist, and crashes result. The more a car demands passivity from its driver and then, in a dangerous instant, expects that driver to resume control (the definition of level 2 automation), the more a driver becomes a consumer – a capitalist subject who pays for the car but is not fully in control of it, even if still responsible for it financially and legally. The perception of car-drivers is now schizoid: on the one hand lies a flattered consumer who has been promised mastery, power, sophistication, and safety by virtue of buying a new car; on the other hand, car-drivers are considered flawed and outmoded, much like the cars designed to quickly become obsolescent or dissatisfying to consumers. There are deep roots to this contradiction. In *Magic Motorways*, Norman Bel Geddes, chief designer of the Futurama exhibit, elaborated on the expressways that were his employer's underlying motive for the spectacle. Bel Geddes described the driver not as a pampered consumer but rather as a weak cog in need of discipline or correction:

> Human beings, even when at the wheel, are prone to talk, wave to their friends, make love, day dream, listen to the radio, stare at striking billboards, light cigarettes, take chances. . . . With the changes in the car, will the driver too be changed? . . . these cars of 1960 and the highways on which they drive will have in them devices which will correct the faults of human beings as drivers. They will prevent the driver from committing errors. They will aid him in passing through intersections without slowing down or causing anyone else to do so and without endangering himself or others. (Bel Geddes, 1940: 48, 56)

Driving, which had been promoted as a pleasure or a privilege, was instead a burden – a task humans performed poorly. In the totalitarian design and paternalist rhetoric of Bel Geddes, a driver's dependence on the car was entrenched by superhighways, even as the driver's competence was cast in doubt by the conditions the expressways created. The goal of Futurama, for its builder GM, was not so much to persuade World's Fair visitors to buy GM cars as to persuade the United States and other nations to build networks of motorways, and by that measure, it was an enormous success. The United States began the Interstate Highway System with the Federal-Aid Highway Act of 1956.

Also in 1956, GM announced a new fantasy for electronically guided automobiles, promoted in a touring car show called Motorama. Hypersonic fighter jets were the acme of US military machismo at the time and the focus of many boyish dreams. GM developed prototype concept cars – the Firebird I, II, III, and IV – powered by gas turbine engines derived from jets. The cars resembled combat aircraft on four wheels, with sharp pointed tails and fins, and bubble-top canopies instead of a roof and windows. The engines operated at nearly 30,000 rpm, with temperatures reaching 1,500 degrees Fahrenheit (Figure 5). A film titled "Key to the Future," produced to promote the Firebird II, featured a new highway diorama and the same visit-to-the-future trope as the 1939 Futurama. In the film, a family of four driving a GM convertible is stuck in traffic on a hot day, and the teenage son tunes the car's radio to a station that takes them to 1976, when they find themselves in the Firebird II, driving on an expressway through the desert southwest. All the film's dialog is in verse, like a campy musical, and the family communicates with a "tower man" or highway traffic controller who directs them, like an aircraft, into a high-speed guided lane for their vacation journey to Chicago. The happy family is sitting in a greenhouse in the desert sun, next to a turbine that the car's dashboard confirms is at 1,400 degrees, so they turn on the air conditioning as dad lights up a cigar. Fantasy perhaps, but in hindsight, it seems like a comic farce.

Silicon Valley tech mogul Peter Thiel, in 2011, delivered a famous quip: "We were promised flying cars, but instead we got 140-character tweets." He was trying to express Silicon Valley's resolve to deliver futuristic yet practical products that would please customers frustrated by the unspectacular innovations of social media platforms like Twitter. Elon Musk, having trashed Twitter, is still trying to deliver the promised cars. The AV, as Tesla and Waymo promise it, is not futuristic; it is nostalgic for the preposterous futurisms of the early space age, such

Figure 5 General Motors concept cars, Firebird II and Firebird III.

as Motorama. Musk's futurism is that of an adolescent weaned on the sci-fi television and comics of the 1960s and 1970s, and his marketing strategy outdoes Sloan's GM in its pace of customer dissatisfaction. Musk's promises come from, and are aimed at, a privileged, urban, affluent, male, and mostly Californian market – a fraternity of tech bros. This form of fetishization of the car reinforces a myth, or rather a false promise, that improvements to the car will solve problems and satisfy desires, when in fact it is the network of automobility that needs to change, particularly in California. "Transportation sufficiency" is the term Peter Norton uses for the antidotes to the car industry's strategy of customer dissatisfaction (Norton, 2021: 3). The vehicles for reducing VMT and CO_2 emissions are already available: smaller, lighter, less powerful, and less expensive cars, shared by more passengers, together with improved bus systems, bike lanes, and affordable high-density housing to reduce lengthy commutes. This message is not futurist; it is practical, incremental, and mundane. It asks for car-drivers to change their behavior and calls for cars that rely on existing technologies, not costly and complex automation.

Norton adds that "the term autonomous vehicle (AV) is paradoxical" because "an AV is controlled by its program just as a conventional car is controlled by its human driver" (4). Without delving into the legal liability of the programmers and the tech giants who employ them, Norton argues, "human decisions will continue to govern the behavior of so-called autonomous vehicles as their capacities improve ... The human decision makers who really drive 'autonomous vehicles' take chances too, because few people would pay for a ride in an AV that takes none" (5). It would be too slow and too cautious to meet the passengers' expectations. AV promoters, such as Musk, keep repeating their techno-futurist fantasies in a manic effort to hide these facts. Tesla's Autopilot software and sensors are incapable of the full automation Musk promises, and even when it becomes more capable, deadly crashes will persist because, if it were programmed for safety, it would make riding in a car even more mundane and boring.

The future of the car-driver hinges on a number of questions: Is the owner or passenger in the AV a powerful, privileged voyager, or a helpless, infantilized prisoner? Does the AV fulfill the sci-fi parable we saw in Section 2? Will self-driving cars render drivers obsolete or redundant? Does the car enslave humans, liberate them, or put them out of work? Was Hiroshi Tamura's claim that "to drive makes us human" wrong after all? Is there a future for the car-driver, the cyborg, or human/machine hybrid that has dominated transportation for more than a century? Or will there only be car-passengers? Is the AV an animated robot that appropriates all the humanist qualities of cars? If so, will this shift return humans to the more self-sufficient, ambulatory lives they practiced for thousands of years before the Anthropocene?

To pose these questions about a representative or abstracted car-driver, or to refer collectively to all car-drivers, is unjust. As of now, only a tiny, wealthy elite can ride in AVs or test out Tesla's Autopilot feature. In a January 2023 article in the *New York Times Magazine* about the crashes involving self-driving Teslas, reporter Christopher Cox accompanied a loyal Tesla owner and driver: "Alford told me that the automotive jargon for anyone on the street who is not in a car or a truck is a 'V.R.U.,' a vulnerable road user. And it's true: Pedestrians and cyclists and children in strollers and women in wheelchairs – they are so fragile compared with these giant machines we've stuffed into our cities." Cox, riding alongside Mr. Alford, describes the scene as the Tesla, in Autopilot mode, attempts to make a left turn:

> Something had gone wrong with the traffic light, which was flashing red, and drivers in all four directions, across eight lanes, had to figure out when to go and when to yield. The choreography here was delicate: There were too many cars to interweave without some allowances being made for mercy and confusion and expediency. Among the humans, there was a good deal of waving others on and attempted eye contact to see whether someone was going to yield or not.
>
> We crept toward the intersection, car by car, until it was our turn. If we were expecting nuance, there was none. Once we had come to a complete stop, the Tesla accelerated quickly, cutting off one car turning across us and veering around another. It was not so much inhuman as the behavior of a human who was determined to be a jerk. (Cox, 2023)

Norton asserts that the software guiding this Tesla should be attributed to the programmers and executives behind it. They are responsible for its behavior. For the road users at that intersection, however, anthropomorphism was instinctual; they were waving and attempting eye contact with the car-driver, but Mr. Alford could not respond. Tesla's autopilot car-driver violated the rules of the civil society of automobility and might also have injured a driver or taken a pedestrian's life.

Behind the software of Autopilot, Waymo, and other AVs are the learning networks that attempt to instrumentalize the experiences and instincts of road users, a process that draws upon not only drivers but nearly all internet users. Uber and Lyft were able to use smart phones and geo-locating software to replace taxi cabs because the consumer had become a cyborg: smart phone plus human body. Road users, whether they drive cars or not, have become interpellated as computer users, as Ben Pettis illustrates in a paper about the reCAPTCHA system devised by Google and used by many websites (Pettis,

2023). The system asks users to identify traffic lights, crosswalks, or motorcycles in a grainy photo. As Pettis explains, these Turing tests are used because, by doing so, Google gets free labor from computer users who interpret images subsequently fed into training data for self-driving car software. By virtue of this task, the internet User (a term Pettis defines as the desirable, profitable internet consumer/customer) is a road user in the system of automobility. Cyberspace is often imagined as an immaterial, parallel universe, but the ubiquity of reCAPTCHA indicates how Google, the internet's largest corporate agent, considers Users to be inhabitants of roadscape. Roadscape is the environment the User comprehends and the reality AVs will inhabit, which means AVs are cyborgs trained on human wisdom about roadscape. In the first Futurama exhibit, the prototypical modern subject/consumer became a car-driver rather than an ambulatory human. In the twenty-first century, the consumer inhabits both cyberspace and roadscape. Roadscape is both private and public, and the User is asked to divulge personal information under the pretense of contributing to the public good, but in fact only to advance the goals of Google's Waymo in its effort to create self-driving cars. When or if the User becomes a passenger or farepayer of those vehicles, the User will be an even more profitable consumer, a captive who can be manipulated into traveling to an advertiser's business and spending money there.

3.2 Customizers as Car Critics: Nostalgia and Irony at Gambler 500

Policymakers and transit activists trying to reduce CO_2 emissions have pinned their hopes on electric cars. These activists, like Motordom's own marketers, aim their messages at dissatisfied car-drivers – those who might buy a more efficient, less polluting model.[2] During the AV boomlet of the 2010s, a smaller set of planners and engineers proclaimed an imminent and massive transition to fleets of electric shared autonomous vehicles that would displace privately owned cars, at least from the cores of major cities, and thereby free up space devoted to parking for more productive uses, such as housing. The Covid-19 pandemic extinguished this futurist scheme, although the huge increase in remote work or telecommuting has reduced traffic congestion in some cities. In 2023–24, the rate of increase in sales of electric cars declined, hinting at the possible limits of consumers' willingness to replace internal combustion engines with batteries (or a recognition of the failure to build a nationwide charging network for those batteries).

---

[2] Motordom, Peter Norton explains, is a "moniker, from the first half of the twentieth century ... for companies and interest groups engaged in efforts to promote automotive transportation and roadbuilding, and is therefore worth reviving" (Norton, 2021: 11–12).

Current conditions in the US market should inspire a study of what types of cars people truly want to drive. In the United States, a vast majority of people depend utterly on their cars for daily routines. The marketing doctrine of customer dissatisfaction assumes that consumers will buy a new car if they can be persuaded that the car they have is not good enough, but it overlooks those who love their cars and don't wish to replace them. The success of GHG emissions reduction efforts hinges on the question: Will a majority of drivers shift to electric cars, or should emphasis be placed instead on reducing VMT and the consumption of petroleum fuels? Recent retreats by Ford and GM from their huge investments in electric car and battery production highlight the significance of the question. Automakers are active in market research, but they cannot easily account for sudden shifts in government policy, as will occur in 2025. Outreach directly to drivers, rather than to politicians and regulators, might be more effective. Activists and analysts fail to perceive how many car enthusiasts also consider themselves critics or reformers of the cars Motordom offers them. Because enthusiasts aim to expose, to satirize, or simply to fix the failings of mass-market cars, activists would be wise to engage with the enthusiasts to make them allies rather than foes, because together the two groups might improve automobility.

I offer as a case study Ed Roth, who, along with George Barris, was among the best-known car artists of the Kustom Kulture movement. In the mid-1950s to early 1960s, Roth designed some of the most bizarre, flamboyant, and parodic celebrity cars, comparable to Barris' original Batmobile. A documentary titled "Tales of the Rat Fink" produced by Ron Mann around the time Roth passed away in 2001, includes interviews with Roth, as well as ventriloquized narratives from some of his cars, whose headlights flash as they speak. In his own voice, Roth recalls his high school life in Bell, CA, in the 1950s as "an outcast, a motorhead" who failed every class except auto shop and art. His first car, at age 14 in 1946, was a 1933 Ford. He and like-minded hot-rodders, some of whom were World War II vets, rebelled against the square, conformist esthetics of the Detroit 3 and its advertising, which aimed at older audiences and emphasized glamorous formal wear and country clubs. The hot-rodders' vernacular counter-esthetic preferred older, simpler, cheaper, pre-war cars as the basis for their mods. Roth built businesses in Los Angeles, first painting pin-striping on clients' cars, then building his own Kustoms and depicting them in cartoons and t-shirts, working alongside fellow car artists Von Dutch and Robert Williams, both employed by Roth's firm. Roth claims to have invented the custom t-shirt, enlivened with sketches of hot-rods driven by animals or demented humans. The Rat Fink character, who became his alter ego, he explains as a reaction to Mickey Mouse, ubiquitous in his neighborhood because Disneyland had recently opened in nearby Anaheim. The 1958–60 Edsel was another provocation because, as many car historians have explained, the claims Ford made for the brand's "revolutionary new design" were so obviously false (Gartman, 1994: 174–181). Around the same time, Roth began to work in fiberglass, which enabled him to build custom – or Kustom – car bodies from scratch rather than modify older models. His first breakthrough was the 1960 Outlaw, who, in the documentary, says: "I wasn't a hotrod, I wasn't a race car," but nonetheless won all the car shows he entered. In car shows, the competitive nature of the hot-rods could be transferred to a new venue in which more enthusiasts could take part. At car shows around the United States today, owners of restored, customized, and hot-rodded cars often convey a rosy nostalgia about the era. The cars are now older than almost all the participants, however, and reflect the era of their parents or grandparents. Show-and-shine events eliminate the danger and rebellion of both hot-rodders and lowriders and provide a marketplace for the t-shirts and other merchandise that supported Roth, Von Dutch, and now support many customizing and tuning brands.

Highbrow studies of the Kustoms, notably Tom Wolfe's *The Kandy-Kolored, Tangerine-Flake Streamline Baby* and John DeWitt's *Cool Cars, High Art*, argued that the Kustoms followed esthetic trends of modernist art. They invoked Tintoretto, Brancusi, and Marcel Duchamp, but the highbrow art history lens is not shared by many car enthusiasts, and even Duchamp misses the satiric genius of an artist like Ed Roth. Tom Wolfe appears in "Tales of the Rat Fink," wearing his trademark white suit and standing next to his stock 2003 white Cadillac – just the kind of car Roth was mocking as ugly and boring. In the film, Roth replies to Wolfe's praise for him as the Salvador Dalí of the Kustom style by asking: "What car did Dalí ever build?"

Roth also explains how he grew tired of street racing because he too often damaged his cars, and so his Kustoms parodied the hot-rod esthetic by exaggerating its exposed engines and chrome accessories. Then, during the early space race, Roth parodied the fantasy of flying cars with his Rotar, a bubble-topped bean-bag shape in red, white, and blue, with two fans intended to make it hover a few inches off the ground.

Kustoms from Roth and Barris parodied both the fantastical visions of Futurama, and the hyper-masculine egotism of hot-rodders. More recently, a Mad Max customizing style has influenced participants in the annual Burning Man festival, alluding to the film franchise's post-apocalyptic collapse of automobility. Many other esthetics and sub-cultures thrive in local regions. Vernacular car customizing is often assumed by folklorists and anthropologists to express ethnic cultures or traditions, based on stereotypes about what kinds of cars are owned and driven by people of various ethnic groups – for example, the

Chicano lowrider, the muscle cars of White hot-rodders, and the Black "ghetto cruiser," which has evolved into variations of lowriders such as the donk and the slab. *The Fast and the Furious*, the first movie in the blockbuster franchise, challenged these stereotypes with its portrayal of street racing clubs or gangs made up of Chicano/Latino, Asian, and White customizer/racers, even though members of all three groups drove similar Japanese-brand tuner cars, a popular style in California at the time the film was made (Beltrán, 2005; Kwon, 2004).

In one of the best-informed essays about car culture by a prominent cultural studies scholar, Paul Gilroy, who identifies himself as a nondriver, writes in "Driving While Black" of his disappointment with how the car has perpetuated apartheid, but also with Black consumerism and R&B and rap artists' penchant for greed and bling. Gilroy appears irked that more Black men don't follow his ethic of protest against automobility. His exception that proves the rule is Bob Marley, who proudly drove a BMW in Jamaica but, in his younger years, had been "working in the US automobile industry producing cars in the Chrysler plant in Wilmington, Delaware." He draws a "portrait of Marley not as anxious, upwardly mobile driver cocooned in a shiny private shell of German techno-aesthetic excellence 'accessorized' with his vanity plates, but as a grumbling and disaffected worker in the auto industry" (Gilroy, 2001: 101). Bob Marley as both car-driver and auto plant worker matches the Fordist approach used by other Marxist cultural critics writing about cars. Gilroy cites André Gorz (93) and discusses how the separation of work from home and suburban white flight were both made possible by the car. He does not, as other academics have done, reify an ethnic cultural identity in Black car customizing.

Stereotypes about car modification and ethnicity are neither deterministic nor functionalist; they are esthetic and creative. A vast majority of those who drive pick-ups do so not because they need such vehicles for their jobs but rather to cultivate a style. Lowriders are non-utilitarian, unable to enter many driveways and parking lots, and for most drivers, big pick-ups are equally impractical. Nearly any car modification genre or esthetic (such as lifted trucks, lowriders, customs, or rat rods) can be applied to nearly any vehicle. A pick-up can be chopped and lowered to become a lowrider, just like an Impala or Monte Carlo. Conversely, a Chevrolet Caprice sedan can acquire a lift kit and 30-inch rims to become a donk. The esthetics are in some senses strict but also flexible. Over time, the esthetic rules emerge dialectically in differentiation from one another. For example, enthusiasts building early lowriders noticed that hot-rods designed for drag racing often had larger rear wheels and tires than the front. A few Chicanos, such as Joaquin Arnett, participated in early hot-rod drag racing (Kerr, 2000: 31–35). Most lowriders did not, however, and they adjusted their suspensions or hydraulics to lift the car's front end higher than the rear.

A related dynamic led lowriders to install undersized rims, such as Daytons, and accompanying small tires for all four wheels, in contrast to the trend among pick-ups to have larger wheels and tires. Then the donk style differentiated from the lowrider by installing hugely oversized rims on similar 1970s to 1990s Detroit 3 sedans, particularly the Chevrolet Caprice.

Regions like Southern California, home to large groups of young people from many ethnic and social backgrounds, foster these dialectics of vernacular customization, whereas isolated settings have more long-term consistency. Research by Alix Roederer on lowriders in Chimayó, New Mexico, concludes that the cars represent continuity rather than resistance, and religious rather than ethnic identity. Informants told Roederer they see lowrider processions as reinventing the parades on horseback traditionally held at El Santuario de Chimayó in the nineteenth century and earlier. The cars move slowly, and the elaborate airbrush paintings on all panels of the cars often display Catholic devotional symbols (Roederer, 2024). The cars are often passed along as family heirlooms, securing pride amidst the hardships of drug addiction and poverty in rural New Mexico.

Whereas the hot-rod, the lowrider, the tuner, and the lifted pick-up are the four most popular car modification esthetics in the United States today, plenty of other styles have a substantial presence in North America, not to mention dozens of others around the world. In recent years, I have followed the emergence of the Gambler 500, a vernacular car modification movement that updates the parodic car modification initiated by the Kustoms. It was founded in Oregon in 2014, and its annual rally is referred to by some as "the redneck Burning Man." I attended the event in Redmond, OR, in June 2024. The esthetic of the Gambler 500 departs from the premise that one should buy a car for $500 or less, get it running, modify it with homemade or found materials, and drive it to the event. In its early years, this was a multi-day rally on a course through the dusty back roads of central Oregon, with overnight camping on remote, undeveloped sites. It is an impromptu, noncompetitive, "no rules" event; and many participants don't observe the $500 limit. Some arrive in their daily drivers, often old vans and wagons; some tow RVs or camp trailers; and some bring their Gambler car on a trailer because it is not street legal, lacks doors, or has no windows. Some who live in Central Oregon drive their Gambler car even if it is not street legal.

The Gambler fan base shares a fondness for car models that have been scorned by others, such as the Pontiac Aztek, Smart Fortwo (Figure 6; Ed Roth claims the design was inspired by his Surfite kustom), Subaru Brat, and fading brands such as Lincoln and Chrysler that once were popular but now are rare, especially in Oregon. The Gambler car is a counter-esthetic that rejects the precision, authenticity, and high cost of both new and restored cars, as well as the fine paint, shiny

Figure 6 A modified Smart Fortwo at Gambler 500, Redmond, Oregon, June 2024

chrome, and pleasing proportions of both Kustoms and lowriders. Car shows that award prizes to the most exacting, thorough restorations or most beautiful paint and striping seem snobbish and exclusive to "Gamblers," who might have acquired and prepared their car during a drunken spree the previous weekend. Their cars sometimes sport decals, handwritten slogans, and graffiti that pastiche race cars with their sponsors' advertisements on them (Figure 7). Because the rally and venue are on gravel and dirt, many Gambler cars are modified with raised suspensions and larger tires, and all get covered in dirt, which enhances the counter-esthetic. The lifted pick-up and monster truck styles, which also emphasize mud and grime, are nonetheless rare at Gambler 500; instead, participants enjoy turning older sedans and coupes, even small sports cars like the Mazda Miata, into dirt road racers. The Gambler 500 stage rally was discontinued in 2022, and racing shifted to a dirt track loop at the Deschutes County Fairgrounds in Redmond, Oregon. The racing format is now called HooptieX, pronounced "hooptiecross," and is a sideline to the camp's live music and parties.

Figure 7 A modified Chevrolet Monte Carlo at Gambler 500. June 2024

The public face and mission of Gambler 500 is to collect trash and abandoned vehicles on public lands and deliver them to landfills. The organization's website boasts of the hundreds of thousands of pounds of trash collected at each event, and the entrance to "Gamblertown," as the camp is sometimes called, features a row of large dumpsters for participants to dispose of what they've collected. A friend who is a US Forest Service ranger in Crescent, Oregon, expressed his support for Gambler 500 and its mission, adding that he recalled no legal issues with the earlier stage rallies and campouts. Gambler 500 captures some of the contradictions of automobility in the Anthropocene. Cars emit GHGs and damage air quality and the livability of neighborhoods, but members can use their special cars to clean up the less visible pollution left on remote public lands. Informal backwoods camping in Oregon includes many people who have no other home than an aging trailer or RV and who cannot afford RV parks. These folks may include some participants in the event, who are responsible for abandoning decrepit RVs that other Gamblers remove from the forest. Gamblers, like many other car-drivers, want to feel they are part of the solution, whether or not they acknowledge they are part of the problem.

Gambler 500 cars often resemble those in dirt track racing, one of the least expensive and most accessible forms of competitive motorsport in the United States. For much of the twentieth century, these events often included demolition derbies, neo-gladiatorial contests where cars in an arena crash into one another until only one remains running. Itai Vardi, in a history of demolition derbies and other spectacles of deliberate car crashes, showed that these competitions were not merely a short-lived sideshow to NASCAR but enjoyed a long history and were performed at major venues such as Soldier Field in Chicago, the Los Angeles Coliseum, and the New York World's Fair. Vardi writes of Sloanism's annual model year redesigns: "the policy of frequent model changes thus must be understood as an index of destruction, not only of production ... manufacturers had to not only physically outmode older cars, but remake consumers' previous desires and tastes by severing their emotional attachments to the dated models as well – a task Vance Packard caustically dubbed in 1960 as 'obsolescence of desirability'" (Vardi, 2011: 27). During the sport's heyday in the 1960s, crash stunt drivers were stars featured in automobile advertising, confirming the industry's complicit desire to destroy old cars in order to sell new ones. Some of the ad spots even promoted these drivers as safety experts. Gambler 500 continues a tradition articulated by the first major promoter of demolition derbies, Ward Beam: "In 1928, he introduced the 'Ash Can Derby.' Dubbing it 'the world's worst race,' Beam called on lay drivers to enter in this event worn-down 'junk-piles, purchased under 50$'" (24).

Taste in popular music is often driven by nostalgia, and in today's streaming era, enjoying old music doesn't require a collection or curation. Cars are at the opposite extreme: expensive and time-consuming restoration and maintenance are needed to relive the experience of driving an old car. The collectors of 1950s and 1960s cars, who, by the time I began doing this research, were aging baby boomers from the hot-rod and muscle car eras, often enhanced the atmosphere at a car show by playing rock-and-roll music of that period. Ford market research, cited by auto industry journalist Keith Bradsher, confirms that the Detroit 3 were aware of how pop music could help sell their products:

> Automotive preferences seem to be a lot like tastes in music: They form early; often in rebellion against parents' tastes, and they last for life. Baby boomers who came of age in the 1960s have never shaken their love of groups like the Beatles, the Grateful Dead and the Rolling Stones. Some of their younger brothers and sisters retain an incomprehensible love of disco music from the 1970s. Similarly, men and women who lusted after big cars in the 1930s and 1940s are still buying large cars today. People seem to form their strongest, most enduring attachments to music and to automobiles between the ages of 12 and 15, Ford officials say. (Bradsher, 2002: 356)

Some of the car songs of the 1960s and 1970s, such as Johnny Cash's "One Piece at a Time," Mose Allison's "V-8 Ford," and Jerry Reed's "Lord, Mr. Ford" were critical of the US auto industry, reflecting an ironic spirit similar to that of the customizers and enthusiasts we just surveyed. Cash grew up in rural Arkansas, graduated from high school in 1950, and moved to Pontiac, Michigan, where he quickly found work in a Fisher body stamping plant (Streissguth, 2007). The opening line, "Well I left Kentucky back in '49, and went to Detroit, work on an assembly line," was adjusted to fit rhyme and meter. The premise of the song is the Fordist principle that laborers in a factory ought to be able to afford to buy the products they build. However, the lyric persona doesn't perceive this as economic justice; he simply shares the Sloanist consumer's desire for the most expensive and prestigious of GM products:

> The first year they had me puttin' wheels on Cadillacs
> Every day I'd watch them beauties roll by
> And sometimes I'd hang my head and cry
> 'Cause I always wanted me one that was long and black.

If Cash had enjoyed the job, he might never have become a country music legend. He lasted less than a month in the stamping plant and enlisted in the US Air Force a couple of weeks after quitting. He took up playing guitar while living on a military base in Germany. The song's persona, however, decides to steal all the necessary parts for his Cadillac "one piece at a time ... with help from my friends" and build his own car, a scheme that keeps him in the factory for an entire career:

> I've never considered myself a thief,
> But GM wouldn't miss just one little piece
> Especially if I strung it out over several years

Because Sloanist design relied on small cosmetic changes every year, when he and his co-conspirator tried to assemble the car more than twenty years after they started collecting parts, "the transmission was a '53 and the motor turned out to be a '73 / And when we tried to put in the bolts all the holes were gone." The assembly line worker, doing one small task over and over, appears not to have noticed design changes in the cars he was building but nonetheless has the skills to make a custom car that is unique and attracts attention. Ed Roth's first successful Kustom, "Outlaw," from 1960 was also a bricolage of parts from various makes, a '55 Caddy engine, the rear end of a '58 Ford, '48 Ford taillights, the windshield from a '27 Dodge, and twin headlights from a '57 Rambler, according to the voice of Outlaw in "Tales of the Rat Fink."

In the song's spoken-word coda, Cash adopts the nasal voice of a CB radio user who identifies himself by the handle "Cotton Mouth in the Psycho-Billy Cadillac." He is evidently proud, not humiliated, to hear the laughter of onlookers and to befuddle the clerks at the DMV, who must assign the car a model year for its registration. When the song was released in 1976, it reached #1 on the country singles chart. Bruce Fitzpatrick, owner of Abernathy Auto Parts and Hilltop Auto

Figure 8 Johnny Cash in the "One Piece at a Time" Cadillac, with builder Bruce Fitzpatrick on the right.

Salvage in Nashville, was asked by promoters to assemble such a car for photographs with Cash and his band members (Figure 8). He did so, but then, after the photo sessions, crushed the car. Another incarnation of the Psycho-Billy Cadillac was commissioned by the Johnny Cash Museum in Nashville, where it is still on display.

Like Johnny Cash, many American consumers had seen the absurdity of Sloanist pseudo-individualization since the 1950s, and market competitors of the Detroit 3 also mocked it as a way to promote their brands as alternative cars. Advertisements for the Volkswagen Beetle in the 1960s emphasized how the model had changed little over decades of production. Spare parts were widely available and affordable, as with the Model T fifty years earlier. One print ad by the famous art director Len Sirowitz showed a Beetle with well-fitting body panels in many different colors. It could have been a reply to the Psycho-Billy Cadillac.

4 Carbolization

I coined this word, a portmanteau combining cars, carbon emissions, and globalization, as a term for how car-dependence is entrenched in modernity, leading to GHG emissions (Sayre, 2020). Here, I want to suggest that carbolization also characterizes the Anthropocene because the autotelic, or self-reinforcing, feedback loops of automobility make it very difficult to reduce (much less escape) car-dependence, much as carbon emissions are exacerbated by feed-back loops, including melting polar ice caps and permafrost. Complicating the problem is the increasing momentum of carbolizing modernity. The shift from roadscapes of mixed transportation modes to expressway monocultures of high-speed cars required longer in the United States than the twenty years promised in the original Futurama. In China, however, it was achieved in roughly two decades, starting in the 1990s. The Chinese had many reasons to be aware of the dangers of car-dependence, chiefly air pollution and climate change, but they saw the car industry as essential to their nation's industrialization, wealth, and pride. The final pages of this section offer some hints as to why this was. First, however, I tell the history of how automobile pollution regulation in the United States began to be enforced by the EPA in Southern California, where car exhaust pollution was most acute. This is a tale with cautionary lessons for climate change, building upon a separate paper (Sayre, 2023) contrasting Fordism with consumerism.

4.1 Air Pollution and Regulation in Los Angeles, 1973

The topography of the Los Angeles region makes it susceptible to severe air pollution. The basin in which the metropolis sits is surrounded by mountains on the north and east sides, and by the Pacific Ocean to the southwest. Cool ocean breezes often clear the air near the beaches, but the mountains and the hot, dry deserts beyond them create high pressure that prevents these winds from moving further inland and dissipating the city's pollution. The result is a temperature inversion; dense, cool air from the ocean creates a layer above the warmer air of the city and traps auto exhaust and other polluted effluents. The inversions can persist for weeks.

In the 1940s and 1950s, armaments and chemical industries that had sprung up during World War II were polluting the air in Los Angeles, and this began to damage residents' health and the popular image of the region. Arie Haagen-Smit, a chemist at the California Institute of Technology in Pasadena, began a series of experiments to determine the constituents of the smog that plagued the basin. The word "smog" was coined from "smoke" and "fog," but in truth, the acrid brownish gas consists of ozone, nitrogen oxides, and unburned hydrocarbons, catalyzed by sunlight in the air (McCarthy, 2008: 118–123; Mondt, 2000: 4–13). Angelinos believed that sun and clear air defined their city, and they did not initially accept that their cars and abundant sunshine were the primary causes of the smog that afflicted them. Aerospace and defense industries employed more workers in Southern California than automobile manufacturers, so regulations imposed on carmakers faced weaker opposition. California would become the leader in regulating harmful emissions in automobile exhaust, a distinction the state still holds in the 2020s.

In the late 1960s, urban California's most serious air pollutants were carbon monoxide, photochemical oxidants, nitrogen dioxide, and hydrocarbons, all prominent in car exhaust. Factories with smokestacks are easy to locate and are popular targets for regulation, unlike the dispersed pollution of automobiles, to which every driver is a contributor. Haagen-Smit held the unenviable task of persuading the state that clearing the air could only be achieved by drastically reducing the pollution coming out of automobile tailpipes. Haagen-Smit's unlikely ally in this task was a French engineer and World War I veteran, Eugène Houdry, who worked for oil refineries in New Jersey and had become concerned about the health effects of air pollution. In 1956, Houdry received a US patent for the catalytic converter, a device installed in automotive exhaust pipes to capture some unburned hydrocarbons and sulfur. Unfortunately, lead in gasoline clogged the catalysts in the devices, rendering them ineffective after fewer than 10,000 miles of use. Lead had been added to gasoline since the 1920s, when Charles Kettering and Thomas Midgley Jr., working for General Motors' research lab in Dayton, Ohio, had patented Tetra Ethyl Lead as a fuel additive that prevented premature combustion or "knock" in high-compression engines (Farber, 2002: 82–86). Houdry knew that the lead additives were no longer necessary to create fuel with an octane rating high enough for the engines in 1950s cars, but the US automakers, of which GM was the largest, continued to endorse leaded fuel and resisted implementing catalytic converters. A few months before his death in 1962, Houdry's company announced an improved catalytic converter that could greatly reduce toxic emissions, and in 1964 the Motor Vehicle Air Pollution Control Board (MVAPC) set out to fulfill a mandate established by California law to approve at least two devices that would reduce emissions. The board certified four such mechanisms; at that time, the catalytic converter was just one concept among several being explored, including Wankel rotary engines to replace pistons and compressed natural gas to replace gasoline (Marx, 1973). The action of the board was an early instance of what lawyer John Bonine called "technology-forcing regulation," whereby regulators break the resistance of profit-driven industrialists to research and implement new products or methods needed to protect consumers and the environment (Bonine, 1975). Haagen-Smit and others on the board saw their action as calling General Motors' bluff. GM still owned half of the Ethyl Corporation, still profited from leaded gasoline, and opposed installing catalytic converters on its cars. Fortunately, in the late 1960s, one GM executive, Ed

Cole, saw the potential of the catalytic converter and confronted the oil industry to demand that lead be eliminated as a gasoline additive (Flink, 1988: 388).

Consider the lessons of the catalytic converter. In 1964, both consumers and regulators in California wanted a device that would allow the same cars and the same fuels to continue to be manufactured, sold, and driven, but to emit fewer pollutants. "Faced with changing their behavior – by driving less – or installing emission control technology on their cars to deal with the chemical causes of smog, Southern Californians turned their eyes toward Detroit" (McCarthy, 2008: 122). The success of the catalytic converter established a consumerist precedent that would be repeated with car safety regulations beginning in the 1970s, and again with GHG emissions in the 2000s. Car-drivers, the auto industry, and policymakers all looked to technical solutions, to engineered modifications to the car, to mitigate the externalities of automobility. In this key instance, California regulators made it a reality.

After the automakers' intransigence was exposed, smart politicians no longer believed claims that no engineering solution was available to meet a regulatory demand (such as air bags to improve crash safety or hybrid drivetrains to improve fuel efficiency). When consumer advocate Ralph Nader learned of the MVAPC board's announcement, he got in touch with board member S. Smith Griswold and Los Angeles County Supervisor Kenneth Hahn to discuss filing lawsuits against the Detroit 3 automakers. Nader planned to argue in court that automakers were conspiring to delay the implementation of emissions control devices such as the catalytic converter. Nader saw a precedent for this behavior because California regulators had, in 1961, mandated an earlier engine innovation – the PCV valve – on all new cars sold in California. The PCV valve reduced unburned fuel emissions by re-routing part of the exhaust stream back into the combustion chambers. Detroit automakers grudgingly installed them on all vehicles, whether sold in California or elsewhere. Thus, Haagen-Smit, Nader, and others sensed the industry was repeating its stalling tactics with the more sophisticated, costly, and effective catalytic converters (Esposito, 1970: 40–47). Setting aside the doctrines of early Fordism, Nader's movement presented the interests of consumers as opposed to, not aligned with, the interests of corporations, their employees, and stockholders. It also helped make California a proving ground for automobile emissions regulation, a source of policy concepts that later spread to the United States as a whole and to other nations.

Ralph Nader soon became famous for his bestselling book *Unsafe at Any Speed,* published in 1965. Most of the book concerns safety defects and poor designs of cars made by the Detroit 3, but one chapter addresses polluting emissions, drawing upon Nader's collaboration with Los Angeles researchers and activists. In *Unsafe at Any Speed* the car becomes an agent mediating between the corporation that manufactured and marketed it and the consumer who has placed faith and money in it. The best-known part of the book is the opening exposé of the 1960–64 Chevrolet Corvair, a rear-engine, air-cooled model that GM designed as a response to the growing popularity of the Volkswagen Beetle. The rear suspension of the Corvair used a crude swing-axle design, which allowed the camber of the wheels to change as the car rounded curves, and many crashes resulted when a rear tire tucked under and caused the car to roll over, even at moderate speeds. Nader described the scene as if the car were a gothic monster: "In ways wholly unique, the Corvair can become an aggressive, single-minded machine ... Rim scrapings or gouge marks on the road have become the macabre trademark of Corvairs going unexpectedly out of control" (Nader, 1965: 33). GM's response to internal critics of the design was not to install a simple anti-roll bar (such as those used in many other car suspensions) but instead to advise buyers to inflate the front tires to a lower pressure than the rear tires – a directive unique to this model and inconsistent with the recommendations of tire manufacturers. In this melodrama, consumers are portrayed as passive creatures of habit who cannot be expected to learn new habits or skills to protect themselves. Instead, consumers interact only with products, such as the Corvair, and products can be wily, deceptive, unpredictable characters that do not care for their owners as strongly as owners care for the cars. Nader and other muckraking journalists wrote in a melodramatic style; they relished exposing the nefarious deeds of capitalists who seduced and betrayed consumers. The ethical and legal arguments Nader made in the book helped to bring about key environmental protection laws in the US Congress over the following decade. Unfortunately, his appeal relied on an unrealistic premise: consumers' behavior need not change, because the products – and the companies making and selling them – were at fault.

Nader's consumer protection movement has succeeded, as evidenced by the dozens of safety recalls announced by car manufacturers every year. However, this form of consumerism reifies defective or dangerous products rather than considering the consumer and product as interactive agents, such as car-drivers who are responsible for social and environmental problems. A car's driver and its passengers benefit from personal transport, while others external to the car suffer from the GHG emissions, traffic congestion, the lost space consumed by highways and parking lots, and the increased risk of collisions and injuries, among other ills. Consumer activism on behalf of car owners often does little to alleviate these externalities. Making a car safer by installing air bags, anti-lock brakes, warning chimes, and adaptive cruise control in new cars of the 2020s may reduce risks for that car's occupants but does less to protect pedestrians and other VRUs. Car crash fatalities in the United States have risen steadily since

2015, with deaths among pedestrians, bicyclists, and motorcyclists growing faster than those of car-drivers, even as some European countries have seen continuing improvements in road safety (Badger & Parlapiano, 2023).

The catalytic converter was a greater benefit to the public than other devices that safety and emissions regulations have brought to cars since such regulations began, with California's leadership, in the early 1960s. The "cats," as they are informally known, were installed on more than 85 percent of 1975 model year cars sold, leading to reductions of unburned hydrocarbons by 83 percent, carbon monoxide by 83 percent, and nitrogen oxides by 11 percent from those vehicles (McCarthy, 2002: 189). In the next five years, automotive engineers at the Detroit 3 collaborated with Volvo to develop a three-way catalytic converter that also reduced nitrogen oxides. The success of the catalytic converter lay not only in its chemical details but in the structure of air pollution and the car industry. Although cars are dispersed, unlike factories emitting air pollution, they are nearly all manufactured by a few huge corporations, whose grudging agreement to cooperate with regulators quickly changed an entire industry. Reduced pollution is a benefit to all, for there is no rivalry or exclusivity in the consumption of air, to use economists' terms. One person breathing does not reduce the air available to others, and no one is obliged to pay for what they breathe. Everybody in a regional airshed benefits from such emission controls, whether or not they come into contact with any particular car. And whereas many recent safety features have been introduced as extra-cost options, the catalytic converter was mandated for nearly all new cars beginning with the 1975 model year.

Ralph Nader's influence and skills as an activist went beyond the consumerist ideology initiated with his work advocating for the catalytic converter and opposing the Corvair. Nader sought to extend the concept of price fixing, whereby corporate interests collude rather than compete on price, to "product fixing," whereby the major automakers colluded to hold back safety and emission control features from their cars. He argued that a collaboration among the automakers to develop emission control technologies, known as the Inter-Industry Emission Control Program or IIEC, was, in truth, a plan to collude and delay the adoption of devices such as the catalytic converter. In 1969, US Attorney General John Mitchell, appointed by President Richard Nixon, reached a consent decree and an out-of-court settlement; automobile manufacturers promised not to withhold emissions control technology henceforth, and all the evidence the grand jury had collected was sealed.

Many saw the outcome as a cover-up. The automakers were able to hide evidence of their wrongdoing and avoid a public trial. A research group formed by Ralph Nader, the Center for the Study of Responsive Law, published a lengthy report in 1970 entitled *Vanishing Air*, which stoked suspicion that the consent decree was indeed a cover-up of criminal collusion. On top of the suspicions aroused by the investigation, smog that choked Southern California, New York, Philadelphia, and Washington, DC, in the summer of 1970 provoked protests from members of Congress. Public alarm about air pollution was at a high point, and political habits shifted. President Nixon, a pro-business Republican, oversaw the creation of the EPA in December of that year and encouraged a Congress led by liberal Democrats to write and pass some of the strongest environmental protection laws the United States has ever seen. There is no space here to explain the full sequence of legislation on air quality since the early 1960s, but the most important were amendments to the Clean Air Act, written largely by Senator Edmund Muskie of Maine, which passed the House 375–1 and the Senate 73–0 in the summer of 1970. The amended act set a strict timeline for every city and state to reduce the number of days per year that ambient air exceeded limits for each of a list of major pollutants and to draft detailed plans for how to reduce pollution. The EPA and its administrator, William Ruckelshaus, were granted extraordinary powers to enforce the law. As legal scholar Eli Chernow explains:

> The EPA Administrator was to review all implementation plans, rejecting those plans or parts thereof which failed to meet the Act's requirements. In addition, the Administrator had the explicit affirmative duty of promulgating substitute plans, or parts of plans, when the plans submitted were found to be insufficient. (Chernow, 1973: 541)

In Southern California over the next two years, the strict provisions of the law came up against the realities of automobility in a confrontation that is not widely remembered more than fifty years later but carries important lessons for today's efforts to limit GHG emissions. The Southern California Air Resources Board, still chaired by Arie Haagen-Smit, was tasked with drafting an implementation plan by January 1972 that would enable the region to meet the air quality standards. Los Angeles County had exceeded the limits for photochemical oxidants on 241 days out of 365 in 1970. Catalytic converters had not yet been mandated, and so there was no assurance that an engineering fix to cars would enable Americans to continue driving inefficient vehicles while breathing healthy air. On the other hand, Los Angeles politicians, including Kenneth Hahn, did not wish to implement even modest efforts to reduce driving, such as new taxes on gasoline and parking, which they knew would arouse fierce backlash. The EPA itself commissioned a study in Los Angeles predicting that "even a free rapid transit system that got all Angelinos where they wanted to go as fast as the automobile would reduce automobile VMT (vehicle miles traveled) by only 10 percent" (McCarthy, 2002: 205). Hahn and other California leaders believed the confrontation could be productive, however, if it forced the automakers to deliver on their promises. EPA chief William Ruckelshaus knew the law demanded he reject the plan the CARB had submitted, but he also expected Congress to recognize how ambitious – or rather impossible – the 1970 Clean Air Act amendments were, and to quickly revise the law. From January to November 1973, the EPA, acting through Ruckelshaus, presented three alternative plans for the South Coast Air Basin. The first and most draconian was based on an estimate that the air would become clear if gasoline consumption were reduced by 80 percent through a rationing program. Public hearings concerning this plan enabled Los Angelinos to vent their outrage and allowed the EPA to then adopt a conciliatory posture. A second and a third alternative withdrew the threat of gasoline rationing and offered additional detail on the transportation plans, such as dedicated bus and carpool lanes on freeways and surface streets, as well as steep taxes on parking to fund improved bus service. Ruckelshaus called it "a national test case in the willingness of citizens to alter lifestyles to meet air quality standards" (McCarthy, 204).

The lessons of Los Angeles' air pollution from automobiles offer a first chapter in the ongoing tragedy of carbolization. Carbon dioxide and methane are, in some respects, a new type of pollution, emitted from both natural and anthropogenic sources and subject to complex feedback loops involving vegetation, weather patterns, ocean currents, and other factors. With respect to the world's 1.4 billion automobiles and their GHG emissions, the same problems of externalities and consumer behavior arise now as when the EPA and the Clean Air Act confronted Southern California smog in 1973. Drivers still don't want to change their behavior, and they still expect a technological fix for cars that will solve the latest environmental threat.

The story of how American activists, politicians, regulators, and consumers confronted the smog caused by auto emissions in Southern California might be seen as an anticipation, on a small scale, of the political efforts to address GHGs and climate change at the United Nations Global Climate Change conferences in Rio de Janeiro, Paris, and Glasgow. There was a similar dialectic at those meetings between a high-minded resolve to protect human lives and health and a bitter backlash as consumers and politicians, who had hoped or tried to shift the burden onto others, faced the reality of enormous and immediate changes to their daily habits. The analogy with the current politics of GHG emissions falls short, however, when one considers the astonishing success of the catalytic converter compared to the difficulty of reducing GHG emissions. Toxic pollutants in auto exhaust have declined more than 90 percent from the levels in the pre-emission control era in the countries where emissions regulations are enforced. On this score, the comparison with GHG emissions today is untenable. Carbon dioxide emissions are an inevitable product of burning fossil fuels or even organic material such as wood. Methane is a by-product not only of fossil fuel extraction but also of agriculture and the melting of permafrost in polar regions. The equivalent of a catalytic converter to control carbon dioxide emissions would be a device attached to exhaust pipes that filtered out and transformed carbon into a solid before it could combine with oxygen. The carbon could then be buried to prevent oxidation. Even if this were chemically possible, on long trips the bulk and weight of the carbon payload could displace passengers and freight in cars and trucks.

Notwithstanding these fundamental differences between the story of auto emissions control and of GHG emissions from the same transport sources, some lessons can be drawn from the thought experiment:

First, the current method of imposing "technology-forcing regulations" on cars is much the same as the one devised in the 1960s. In the European Union, carbon dioxide emissions from new cars and trucks are measured and limited through a corporate average fuel economy scheme similar to that first used in the United States for fuel economy in the 1970s. Hybrid and electric vehicles are incentivized through the credits and penalties levied on manufacturers and consumers who buy cars. Behavioral and urban planning measures that were so harshly rejected in Los Angeles, such as rationing gasoline, taxing parking fees and parking lots, or even providing incentives to use public transit, have only rarely succeeded, even in authoritarian regimes like China.

Second, the technocratic expectations invested in the electric car today are, in some ways, equivalent to the humbler catalytic converter of the early 1970s. Electric cars are seen as a magical product that will solve the GHG pollution problem without requiring consumers to drive less, use public transit, or pay punitive taxes on fuel. Government regulations and local pledges issued between 2020 and 2022 call for an end to sales of new gasoline and diesel vehicles within ten to twenty-five years. The evident success of emissions controls in improving air quality in North America, Europe, and now in China provides conceptual and political precedent in support of these plans. Electric cars have indeed improved in range and declined in price since 2010. But consumer appetite for them remains limited, and quickly reducing emissions would require measures that affect the entire fleet of vehicles, not just new ones. Policies such as California's mandate, described at the beginning of this Element, do nothing to change older vehicles. When California issued its implementation plan in 1972, it made optimistic predictions for policies such as retrofitting existing vehicles to run on compressed natural gas, but consumerist ideology prevented regulators from modifying cars and trucks owned by individuals.

Third, the upstream limits and less visible effects of the planned transition to electric cars are rarely recognized, and these evoke the Fordism of the twentieth century. Henry Ford was famous for his insistence on vertical integration of the supply chain for the Model T, buying up forest lands around the Great Lakes to supply the hardwoods from which its wheels and bodies were built, as well as railroads, mines, cargo ships, and even rubber plantations. Elon Musk's Tesla Corporation, as well as GM, are now looking to develop lithium mines in Nevada and Oregon, because that metal is as critical for batteries as platinum and palladium are for catalytic converters. The resources required for new products like electric cars detract from their environmentalist appeal because new mines and processing plants will create new sources of contamination for the air and ground water.

4.2 Car Nationalism, Neo-Fordism, and the Future of the Car-Driver

In Section 3, we considered the styles or esthetics of car modification among different ethnic communities in the United States. Given that background, and the phenomenon of the humanity of the car, let us now consider how mass-market car designs have contributed to nationalist identities and imaginaries in the past eighty years. The most obvious relationship followed from the home origins of major car manufacturers. In the mid twentieth-century US, British, German, French, Italian, Swedish, and Japanese companies had distinct design philosophies, reflecting local car cultures and tastes. Models from the post–World War II economic boom became cultural icons, such as the Mini for Britain, the Citroën 2CV for France, the Fiat 500 for Italy, the Trabant in East Germany, and Chevrolet as the leading brand in the United States for much of that period.

This era also saw the neocolonial globalization of capital and import/export flows. The largest carmakers expanded production facilities into countries like Argentina, Australia, Brazil, India, Iran, and Thailand. The result was a counter-diasporic phenomenon whereby local environments shifted the identities of the source brands and sometimes carried them to greater prominence than the original had enjoyed. The Hindustan Ambassador, built from 1957 to 2014, starting at a plant in West Bengal, India, is perhaps the best example. It was a lightly modified Morris Oxford Series III, a British Motor Corporation (BMC) model built at a plant in Oxford, UK, from 1956 until 1959, when the Series IV version replaced it. The Hindustan version, at its height, held a 70 percent share of the Indian car market and, across nearly sixty years, sold a total of around four million units, whereas the British version sold only about 57,000 and was tainted by BMC's reputation for slow cars of questionable quality. The Hindustan Ambassador's success, beginning a decade after India won independence from the British Empire, and the fondness with which many Indians of the postwar generation regarded it show how cars can embody national imaginaries. The pride of workers at the West Bengal plant and others contributed to this nationalism, as well as training managers and engineers for a domestic Indian car industry, which soon emerged in force and is now dominated by Maruti. As India was the world's second most populous country during this period (and as of 2023 the most populous), the potential market was and is huge. Other cases of adopted immigrant national cars include the Renault 4 as the car of Colombia, introduced there in 1966 and manufactured in a plant near Medellín from 1970 to 1977. The 4 and other Renault models were also assembled in Tunisia and Turkey during that period.

A subsequent stage of car market globalization emerged during what we defined in Section 1 as the post-Fordist era, when Japanese car makers expanded their exports by establishing manufacturing plants in other parts of Asia to compete with the US and European brands in those markets. This trend also reached North America, as major automakers wished to circumvent tariffs and limits on imports, especially for large SUVs popular in the United States. New auto assembly factories were located in anti-union "right-to-work" states in the US South, much like the industry had earlier moved into third-world nations. Since the 1980s, the United Auto Workers (UAW) has consistently tried to unionize the factories south of the Ohio River, both those of the Detroit 3 and of global competitors. Nissan opened an assembly plant in Smyrna, TN, in 1983, followed by other manufacturers in the US South: Toyota in Georgetown, KY, in 1988; BMW in Greer, SC, in 1994; Mercedes-Benz in Vance, AL, in 1997; Honda in Lincoln, AL, in 2001; Hyundai in Montgomery, AL, in 2005; and Volkswagen in Chattanooga, TN, in 2011. The UAW promotes its organizing efforts by highlighting the higher wages its workers receive in unionized plants in the Midwest and Great Lakes regions. A nostalgia for the mid twentieth century, when US union autoworkers were perceived to have secure, living-wage jobs, persists today in disputes over whether these workers are threatened by the increased production of electric vehicles (EVs). EVs supposedly require fewer workers to assemble, although the real problem may be that new factories producing EVs and their batteries may not be covered by existing union Collective Bargaining Agreements, or that Chinese-made EVs imported into the United States could undercut the prices of domestic products.

The 2000s initiated a third stage in which China followed the Neo-Fordist plan of using an automobile industry and its exports to develop an industrial base and rise into the ranks of world financial powers. The Chinese government beginning in the 1990s made a policy of developing its automobile industry and building expressways to accommodate the influx of hundreds of millions of cars. Bicycles and three-wheeled rickshaws were forced off these highways. The Chinese program followed that of Germany in the 1930s, which was interrupted by World War II, in the United States beginning with the Futurama exhibition of 1939–40, and in Europe in general in the post–World War II period. China imitated that pattern, and more directly, the success of the Japanese in the 1980s and of Korean carmakers Hyundai and Kia, who have grown significantly since 2010. Automobility advanced in China at a hypermodern pace. Whereas in the 1980s the state prohibited the private ownership of cars, by 2009 the number of registered vehicles had reached 62 million (still only about a third of the number in the United States), and in the following year, China became both the largest manufacturer and the largest market for new cars. Unsurprisingly, in 2009–10, China also became the nation with the largest share of carbon dioxide emissions. Some estimates suggest that the size of China's car and truck fleet will exceed 500 million by 2050 (Sperling & Gordon, 2009: 205–216). China's car-centric formula for industrialization relied on domestic consumption to a degree far greater than permitted in other sectors of its economy. Chinese citizens can buy cars but cannot own land. Car owners enjoy freedom of movement but have limited freedom of speech or expression. The scheme also has a neocolonial side, with China acting as an imperial center seeking to export its internal combustion cars to the less-developed nations that impose no restrictions on GHG emissions and impose no tariffs because they have no domestic brands. In Africa, for instance, historic connections to British Land Rover or French Peugeot cars of the 1960s and 1970s have been lost as Chinese imports gain market share.

The fourth incarnation of *Futurama*, Peter Norton writes, arrived at a 2010 exposition in Shanghai, for which GM and its Chinese partner SAIC built a pavilion (as in 1939, it was the most popular at the expo) and produced a film entitled *2030 Xing!* depicting "a vehicle that can absorb CO_2 and water molecules in the air and, like an actual leaf, convert them into power for the vehicle" (Norton, 2021: 140). As we saw in the previous section, the claim to sequester CO_2 emitted by the car as it runs is not credible, but because GHG emissions are now acknowledged to be a severe problem for automobility, techno-futurist fantasies must promise solutions. More practically, Chinese automakers are maneuvering to dominate global production of EVs and the batteries to power them, while also seeking to manipulate regulations in other markets. An important but little-known instance of this is the relationship between Tesla and Chinese industrial policy. China developed its car industry by inviting leading carmakers to form joint ventures with Chinese firms. Tooling from a failed Volkswagen plant in Westmoreland, Pennsylvania, was shipped to Changchun, Jilin province, and a version of the Jetta sedan renamed the Santana became the bestselling model in China (Hessler, 2005). Gradually, the Chinese partners acquired expertise, copied designs, and caught up to the foreign brands. As air pollution became severe in the 2010s, China imposed emissions regulations that resemble those in the United States and Europe – a CAFÉ-like system whereby manufacturers of internal combustion cars buy credits or surpluses from manufacturers of hybrid or electric cars, who meet the standards with room to spare.

Tesla was already an expert at exploiting these regulations in the United States, specifically in California. Since 2008, Tesla "has earned cash under the state's emissions mandate by selling credits to automakers that could not meet pollution targets. Those credits were worth $3.71 billion by late 2023, according to Gov. Gavin Newsom's office." Tesla executives traveled to China, and "in 2015, at a clean transportation conference in California, Chinese central government officials listened as a Tesla lobbyist laid out the reasons that Beijing should adopt an emissions mandate" which was finalized in 2017. "That change directly benefited Tesla, bringing in an estimated hundreds of millions of dollars in profits" as it sold emissions credits to Chinese automakers. Tesla built its second major factory near Shanghai and was able to overturn the policy China had enforced since the 1980s of forcing foreign automakers to form joint ventures with Chinese companies: "in 2018 officials revoked the rule for all foreign electric car companies" (Hvistendahl, Ewing, & Liu, 2024). Chinese carmakers (like BYD) and battery manufacturers (such as CATL) mimicked Tesla's success. So, as the United States and European Union are accusing China of unfairly subsidizing the EV and battery industries and of selling the cars at predatory low prices, one should not ignore how US and European leaders subsidized Tesla, which could have gone bankrupt in the mid-2010s if not for the revenue derived from tax-credits, low-interest federal loans, and selling CAFÉ emissions credits (Niedermeyer, 2019).

Regulations intended to promote the electrification of automobility and reduce GHG emissions can too easily be distorted by the corporate interests of car manufacturers, and geopolitical rivalries and protectionist policies often exacerbate these trends, while contributing to the wasteful overproduction of cars. Higher taxes on fuels and on vehicle registrations are more direct, more efficient, and equitable ways to reduce VMT. Congestion pricing in urban areas is another targeted method for improving air quality and supporting public transit. While some car lovers may oppose these policies, a better-informed car-driver should recognize the principle articulated by André Gorz, that the car is a privilege that loses its value if it becomes the only mode of transport. Car enthusiasts should be perceptive critics of the car industry and should maintain and repair their vehicles rather than junk them in favor of newer, more expensive models. Local car cultures can also resist the neocolonial and techno-futurist impulses that try to erase consumers' tastes and usurp control over the vehicles drivers choose. Roadscapes around the world ought to be distinct social and infrastructural environments, each operating by informal rules that guide the civil society of automobility. The roadscape cultures of different countries and environments ought to be different. The civil society of automobility has national and regional grammars or vernaculars. Car-drivers and all road users should learn the habits or rules of the roadscape they inhabit because safety and efficiency cannot be imposed according to any single set of metrics.

Similarly, carbolization should not be understood as a relentless progression toward faster transport and infrastructure, but as a dialectic that generates friction and resistance. Cities that have instituted bike-share networks, integrated public transit with micromobility, and congestion pricing for cars, such as London, Paris, Amsterdam, and New York, are often those where cars emerged first. Among latecomers to carbolization, Chinese cities like Beijing and Shanghai have recently taken steps to reverse policies that favored cars and expressways over bicycles (Sayre, 2020: 93–94). Even some less wealthy mega-cities, such as Bogotá, Colombia, have been able to design transport systems that facilitate growing populations, serve the needs of working people in their dense neighborhoods, and limit the dominance of private cars (Kimmelman, 2023).

The car-driver is a hybrid assemblage that many humans have adopted with enthusiasm, and most with tacit, unconscious consent. For the latter group, it is a mundane, semi-conscious activity that invites minimal self-reflection, and even scholars who pride themselves on critical thinking have rarely turned their critique toward their own role as car-drivers. I hope this Element might provoke car-drivers to become more aware of what their habits cost society, the environment, and their own health. Car-drivers need to recognize the degree to which their own humanity has been invested, projected, and ceded to their cars. Then they might be able to reclaim the need for flexible, diverse modes of human movement and collective transit.

References

Adorno, T. 1941. On Popular Music. *Zeitschrift für Sozialforschung* 9(1), 17–48.

———. 1951. *Minima Moralia*. Trans. D. Redmond, 2005. www.marxists.org/reference/archive/adorno/1951/mm/index.htm.

Adorno, T., and M. Horkheimer. 1944. *Dialektik der Aufklärung*. Trans. J. Cumming as *Dialectic of Enlightenment*. New York: Continuum, 1988.

Alpers, G. W., and A. B. M. Gerdes. 2006. Another Look at "Look-Alikes": Can Judges Match Belongings with Their Owners? *Journal of Individual Differences* 27(1): 38–41.

Badger, E., and A. Parlapiano. 2022. The Exceptionally American Problem of Rising Roadway Deaths. *The New York Times*, November 27, 2022, accessed February 4, 2023.

Beckmann, J. 2001. Automobility – A Social Problem and Theoretical Concept. *Environment and Planning D: Society and Space* 19: 593–607. https://doi.org/10.1068/d222t.

Bel Geddes, N. 1940. *Magic Motorways*. New York: Random House.

Beltrán, M. C. 2005. The New Hollywood Racelessness: Only the Fast, Furious, and Multiracial Will Survive. *Cinema Journal* 44(2): 50–67.

Bonine, J. 1975. The Evolution of "Technology-Forcing" in the Clean Air Act. *Envir. Rptr. Monograph*.

Bradsher, K. 2002. *High and Mighty: SUVs – The World's Most Dangerous Vehicles and How They Got That Way*. New York: Public Affairs.

Braidotti, R. 2002. *Metamorphoses: Towards a Materialist Theory of Becoming*. Cambridge: Polity.

Bright, B. 1998. "Heart Like a Car": Hispano/Chicano Culture in Northern New Mexico. *American Ethnologist* 25(4): 583–609. https://doi.org/10.1525/ae.1998.25.4.583.

Chernow, E. 1973. Implementing the Clean Air Act in Los Angeles: The Duty to Achieve the Impossible. *Ecology Law Quarterly* 4(3): 537–581.

Clynes, M. E., and N. S. Kline. 1960. Cyborgs and Space. *Astronautics* 5(9): 26–27, 74–76.

Cox, C. 2023. Elon Musk's Appetite for Destruction. *The New York Times Magazine*, January 17.

Dan Neil Interviews Peter Horbury. 2012. "When Will Chinese Car Design Emerge onto the World Stage?" YouTube Video. The Wall Street Journal. https://youtu.be/Hw2SAxbh5I8?si=FcFZhu7m6y8T9xXi.

References

Dant, T. 2005. The Driver-Car. *Theory, Culture & Society* 21: 61–79. https://doi.org/10.1177/0263276404046061.

——— 2009. True Automobility. In Penny Harvey, Eleanor Conlin Casella, Gillian Evans, et al., eds., *Objects and Materials: A Routledge Companion*. Oxford: Abingdon, 251–259.

Dant, T., and P. J. Martin. 2001. By Car: Carrying Modern Society. *Ordinary Consumption* 44: 143–157.

DeWitt, J. 2002. *Cool Cars, High Art: The Rise of Kustom Kulture*. Jackson: University of Mississippi Press.

Dodge, P. 1996. *The Bicycle*. Paris: Flammarion.

Donnelly, N., ed. 2000. *Customized: Art Inspired by Hot Rods, Low Riders and American Car Culture*. Boston: Harry N. Abrams and The Institute for Contemporary Art.

Edensor, T. 2004. Automobility and National Identity: Representation, Geography and Driving Practice. *Theory, Culture & Society* 21: 101–120.

Eisenberg, E. 1998. *The Ecology of Eden*. New York: Knopf.

Esposito, J. & L. J. Silverman. 1970. *Vanishing Air: The Ralph Nader Study Group Report on Air Pollution*. New York: The Study Group.

Farber, D. 2002. *Sloan Rules: Alfred P. Sloan and the Triumph of General Motors*. Chicago University Press.

Flink, J. 1988. *The Automobile Age*. Cambridge, MA: MIT Press.

Flint, J. M. 1970. GM Sees Autos Fume-Free by '80. *The New York Times*, January 15. Accessed July 27, 2022.

Ford, H., and S. Crowther. 1923. *My Life and Work*. Garden City: Doubleday.

——— 1926. *Today and Tomorrow*. rpt. Cambridge: Productivity Press, 1988.

Furness, Z. 2010. *One Less Car: Bicycling and the Politics of Automobility*. Philadelphia: Temple University Press.

Gartman, D. 1994. *Auto Opium: A Social History of American Automobile Design*. New York, Routledge.

Gasnier, M. 1977. Colombia 1970–1976: Renault 4, the First "Colombian Car," Brings the Car to the Masses. https://bestsellingcarsblog.com/1977/03/. Accessed October 23, 2024.

Gauthier, I., P. Skudlarski, J. C. Gore, and A. W. Anderson. 2000. Expertise for Cars and Birds Recruits Brain Areas Involved in Face Recognition. *Nature Neuroscience* 3: 191–197. https://doi.org/10.1038/72140.

Gendron, T. 1986. Theodor Adorno Meets the Cadillacs. In T. Modleski, ed., *Studies in Entertainment*, Bloomington: University of Indiana Press, 18–30.

General Motors. 1940. "To New Horizons." YouTube Video. U.S. Auto Industry channel. https://youtu.be/aIu6DTbYnog?si=AiN1h26EbFaVibrV.

General Motors and SAIC. May 2011. "2030 Xing!" YouTube Video. https://youtu.be/E995187QoEI?si=WHI83hJ9P6Tg62uF.

General Motors Corporation. 1956. "Key to the Future." YouTube Video. CBS Sunday Morning Channel https://youtu.be/F2iRDYnzwtk?si=z-5SfONdLqma1jXs.

Gertten, F. "Bikes vs. Cars" 2015. dir. F. Gertten. https://vimeo.com/ondemand/bikesvscars/139735099.

Gilroy, P. 2001. Driving While Black. In D. Miller, ed., *Car Cultures*, Oxford: Berg, 81–104.

Goddard, Y. 2002. Grammatical Gender in Algonquian. In *Papers of the 33rd Algonquian Conference*. Winnipeg: University of Manitoba, 195–231.

Gorz, A. 1973. l'Idéologie sociale de la bagnole. Trans. P. Vigderman and J. Cloud, The Social Ideology of the Motorcar. In *Ecology as Politics*. Boston: South End, 1980.

Gramsci, A. 1971. *Selections from the Prison Notebooks*. New York: International.

Haraway, D. 1985. A Cyborg Manifesto : Science, Technology, and Socialist-Feminism in the Late Twentieth Century. In *Simians, Cyborgs, and Women: The Reinvention of Nature*. New York: Routledge, 1991.

Haraway, D. 2008. *When Species Meet*. Minneapolis: University of Minnesota Press.

Harvey, D. 1990. *The Condition of Postmodernity: An Enquiry into the Origins of Cultural Change*. Cambridge: Blackwell.

Hayes, H. 1904. U.S. Patent #777369. Washington D.C.

Hessler, P. 2005. Car Town: An Upstart Automaker Targets the American Markert. *The New Yorker*, September 26.

Hvistendahl, M., J. Ewing, & J. Liu, 2024. *A Pivot to China Saved Elon Musk. It also Binds him to Beijing*. New York: The New York Times.

Jenemann, D. 2007. *Adorno in America*. Minneapolis: University of Minnesota Press.

Keeler, K. 2021. Before Colonization (BC) and after Decolonization (AD): The Early Anthropocene, the Biblical Fall, and Relational Pasts, Presents, and Futures. *Environment and Planning E: Nature and Space*. https://doi.org/10.1177/25148486211033087.

Keiller, P. 2002. Sexual Ambiguity and Automotive Engineering. In J. Kerr and P. Wollen, eds., *Autopia: Cars and Culture*. London: Reaktion, 342–353.

Kerr, L. M. 2000. *Driving Me Wild*. Los Angeles: Juno.

2000. Garage Wall to Gallery Hall: High Art in Lowbrow Society. In N. Donelly, ed., *Customized*, 26–31.

Kimmelman, M. 2023. How One City Tried to Solve Gridlock for Us All. *The New York Times*, December 7, Accessed January 13, 2025.

Kimmerer, R. W. 2015. *Braiding Sweetgrass: Indigenous Wisdom, Scientific Knowledge and the Teachings of Plants*. Minneapolis: Milkweed.

Kwon, S. A. 2004. Autoexoticizing: Asian-American Youth and the Import Car Scene. *Journal of Asian-American Studies* 7(1): 1–26.

Latour, B. 1996. *Aramis, or the Love of Technology*. Trans. C. Porter. Cambridge, MA: Harvard University Press.

Luke, T. 1996. Liberal Society and Cyborg Subjectivity: The Politics of Environments, Bodies, and Nature. *Alternatives* 21(1): 1–30.

Lupton, D. 1999. Monsters in Metal Cocoons: "Road Rage" and Cyborg Society. *Body & Society* 5(1): 57–72.

Malm, A., and A. Hornborg. 2014. The Geology of Mankind? A Critique of the Anthropocene Narrative. *The Anthropocene Review* 11: 62–69.

Mann, R. 2006. "Tales of the Rat Fink." Films We Like.

Marx, W. 1973. Los Angeles and Its Mistress Machine. *Bulletin of the Atomic Scientists* 29(4): 44–48.

Maxim, H. 1936. *Horseless Carriage Days*. New York: Harper & Brothers.

McCarthy, T. 2008. *Auto Mania: Cars, Consumers, and the Environment*. New Haven: Yale University Press.

McShane, C. 1994. *Down the Asphalt Path: The Automobile and the American City*. New York: Columbia University Press.

Miller, D. 2001. *Car Cultures*. Oxford: Berg.

Miller, J. A. 1941. *Fares, Please! From Horse-Cars to Streamliners*. New York: D. Appleton-Century.

Mondt, J. R. 2000. *Cleaner Cars: The History and Technology of Emission Control since the 1960s*. Warrendale, PA.

Nader, R. 1965. *Unsafe at Any Speed: The Designed-In Dangers of the American Automobile* New York: Grossman.

National Highway Traffic Safety Administration, 2024. Traffic Safety Facts. Early Estimate of Traffic Safety Fatalities in 2023. Washington, DC: NHTSA.

New York Times. 1872. The Horse Plague: Fifteen Thousand Horses in this City Unfit for Use. October 25.

Newsom, G. 2020. Statement announcing Executive Order N-79–20. gov.ca.gov/2020/09/23.

Niedermeyer, E. 2019. *Ludicrous: The Unvarnished Story of Tesla Motors*. Dallas: BenBella.

Norton, P. 2021. *Autonorama: The Illusory Promise of High-Tech Driving*. Washington, DC: Island.

Olmsted, F. L., and C. Vaux, 1868. *Observations on the Progress of Improvements in Street Plans, with Special Reference to the Park-Way Proposed to Be Laid-Out in Brooklyn.* Brooklyn: I. Van Anden.

Packard, V. 1960. *The Waste Makers.* New York: David McCay.

Parmesan, C., H. -O. Pörtner, D. C. Roberts, et al. 2022. Terrestrial and Freshwater Ecosystems and Their Services. In H.-O. Pörtner, D. C. Roberts, M. Tignor, et al., eds., *Climate Change 2022: Impacts, Adaptation, and Vulnerability.* Contribution of Working Group II to the Sixth Assessment Report of the Intergovernmental Panel on Climate Change. Cambridge: Cambridge University Press, 197–377, Figure 2.12. 2.13, https://doi.org/10.1017/9781009325844.004.

Paterson, M. 2007. *Automobile Politics: Ecology and Cultural Political Economy.* Cambridge: Cambridge University Press.

Pettifer, J. and N. Turner. 1984. *Automania: Man and the Motor Car.* London: Collins.

Pettis, B. 2023. reCAPTCHA Challenges and the Production of the Ideal Web User. *Convergence: The International Journal of Research into New Media Technologies* 29: 886–900.

Porter, R. C. 1999. *Economics at the Wheel: The Costs of Cars and Drivers.* San Diego: Academic.

Randell, R. 2016. The Microsociology of Automobility: The Production of the Automobile Self. *Mobilities.* https://doi.org/10.1080/17450101.2016.1176776.

Roederer, A. 2024. Sacred Hearts and Sacred Cars: The Visual Culture of Latinx Low Riders. Presentation, American Folklore Society Conference, Albuquerque.

Sayre, G. 2020. "Carbolization": Cars, Carbon Emissions, and the Global Discipline of Automobility. In T. Konrad, ed., *Accelerating Ride to Global Crisis: Transportation and the Culture of Climate Change.* Morgantown: West Virginia University Press, 83–101.

2020. The Humanity of the Car: Automobility, Agency, and Autonomy. *Cultural Critique* 107: 122–147.

2023. Fordism in Detroit, Consumerism in Los Angeles: A Brief History of Automobile Emissions Regulation and Lessons for Greenhouse Gas Pollution. In T. Konrad, C. Mitchell, and S. Schaufler, eds., *Imagining Air: Cultural Axiology and the Politics of Invisibility.* Exeter: University of Exeter Press, 37–55.

Scherr, E. 2024. Automotive Omakase. *Car & Driver* May/June: 76–81.

Sehgal, P. 2024. Who's Afraid of Judith Butler? May 6. www.newyorker.com/magazine/2024/05/06/judith-butler-profile.

Settis, B. 2019. Rethinking Fordism. In F. Antonini, ed., *Revisiting Gramsci's Notebooks*. Lieden: Brill, 376– 387. https://doi.org/10.1163/97890044 17694_023.

Shaeffer, R. & Sims R. Transport. In *Climate Change 2014: Mitigation of Climate Change. Contribution of Working Group III to the Fifth Assessment Report of the Intergovernmental Panel on Climate Change*, 608. https://archive.ipcc.ch/report/ar5/authors.php?q=3&p=8.

Sheller, M., and J. Urry. 2000. The City and the Car. *International Journal of Urban and Regional Research* 24(4): 737–757.

Smith, U. 1899. U.S. Patent #30551. Washington, DC.

Sorensen, C., and S. T. Williamson. 1956. *My Forty Years with Ford*. Detroit: Wayne State University Press, 2006.

Sperling, D., and D. Gordon. 2009. *Two Billion Cars: Driving toward Sustainability*. Oxford: Oxford University Press.

Streissguth, M. 2007. *Johnny Cash: The Biography*. Philadelphia: Da Capo.

Urry, J. 2006. Inhabiting the Car. *Sociological Review* 54: 17–31. https://doi.org/10.1111/j.1467-954X.2006.00635.x.

John. 2004. The "System" of Automobility. *Theory, Culture & Society* 21: 25–39. https://doi.org/10.1177/0263276404046059.

Vardi, I. 2011. Auto Thrill Shows and Destruction Derbies, 1922–1965: Establishing the Cultural Logic of the Deliberate Car Crash in America. *Journal of Social History* 45(1): 20–46.

Veblen, T. 1899. *The Theory of the Leisure Class: An Economic Study of Institutions*. New York: Macmillan.

Windhager, S., D. E. Slice, K. Schaefer, et al. 2008. Face to Face – The Perception of Automotive Designs. *Human Nature* 19: 331–346.

Windhager, S., F. Hutzler, C. C. Carbon, et al. 2010. Laying Eyes on Headlights: Eye Movements Suggest Facial Features in Cars. *Collegium Antropologicum* 34: 1075–1080.

Windhager, S., Bookstein, F., Grammer, K., et al. 2012. "Cars Have Their Own Faces": Cross-Cultural Ratings of Car Shapes in Biological Stereotypical Terms. *Evolution and Human Behavior* 33(2): 109–120. https://doi.org/10.1016/j.evolhumbehav.2011.06.003.

Wolfe, T. 1965. *The Kandy-Kolored, Tangerine-Flake Streamline Baby*. New York: Farrar.

Yeager, P., Szeman, I., Ziser, M., et al. 2011. Editor's Column: Literature in the Ages of Wood, Tallow, Coal, Whale Oil, Gasoline, Atomic Power, and Other Energy Sources. *PMLA* 126(2): 305–326.

Yoon, C. K. 2009. *Naming Nature: The Clash between Instinct and Science*. New York: W. W. Norton.

Acknowledgments

I wish to acknowledge my colleagues Tatiana Konrad at the University of Vienna, Louise Westling and Daniel Wojcik at the University of Oregon, and the Oregon Humanities Center for supporting my research on cars from an environmental humanities and folklore methodology. I also thank two graduate students from the Car Cultures course, Alix Roederer and Linnea Hill, as well as the many undergraduate students who have inspired my research with stories of car modification and enthusiasms in America and around the world: Burkina Faso, Sweden, South Africa, Saudi Arabia, Qatar, China, and India.

Cambridge Elements =

Environmental Humanities

Louise Westling
University of Oregon

Louise Westling is an American scholar of literature and environmental humanities who was a founding member of the Association for the Study of Literature and Environment and its President in 1998. She has been active in the international movement for environmental cultural studies, teaching and writing on landscape imagery in literature, critical animal studies, biosemiotics, phenomenology, and deep history.

Serenella Iovino
University of North Carolina at Chapel Hill

Serenella Iovino is Professor of Italian Studies and Environmental Humanities at the University of North Carolina at Chapel Hill. She has written on a wide range of topics, including environmental ethics and ecocritical theory, bioregionalism and landscape studies, ecofeminism and posthumanism, comparative literature, eco-art, and the Anthropocene.

Timo Maran
University of Tartu

Timo Maran is an Estonian semiotician and poet. Maran is Professor of Ecosemiotics and Environmental Humanities and Head of the Department of Semiotics at the University of Tartu. His research interests are semiotic relations of nature and culture, Estonian nature writing, zoosemiotics and species conservation, and semiotics of biological mimicry.

About the Series

The environmental humanities is a new transdisciplinary complex of approaches to the embeddedness of human life and culture in all the dynamics that characterize the life of the planet. These approaches reexamine our species' history in light of the intensifying awareness of drastic climate change and ongoing mass extinction. To engage this reality, Cambridge Elements in Environmental Humanities builds on the idea of a more hybrid and participatory mode of research and debate, connecting critical and creative fields.

Cambridge Elements

Environmental Humanities

Elements in the Series

Deep History, Climate Change, and the Evolution of Human Culture
Louise Westling

Climate Change Literacy
Julia Hoydis, Roman Bartosch and Jens Martin Gurr

Anthroposcreens: Mediating the Climate Unconscious
Julia Leyda

Aging Earth: Senescent Environmentalism for Dystopian Futures
Jacob Jewusiak

Blue Humanities: Storied Waterscapes in the Anthropocene
Serpil Oppermann

Nonhuman Subjects: An Ecology of Earth-Beings
Federico Luisetti

Indigenous Knowledge and Material Histories: The Example of Rubber
Jens Soentgen

The Open Veins of Modernity: Ecological Crisis and the Legacy of Byzantium and Pre-Columbian America
Eleni Kefala

Slime: An Elemental Imaginary
Simon C. Estok

Growing Hope: Narratives of Food Justice
Alexa Weik von Mossner

Descartes and the Non-Human
Emma Gilby

Automobility and the Anthropocene: The Car as Post-Human
Gordon M. Sayre

A full series listing is available at: www.cambridge.org/EIEH

For EU product safety concerns, contact us at Calle de José Abascal, 56–1°, 28003 Madrid, Spain or eugpsr@cambridge.org.

www.ingramcontent.com/pod-product-compliance
Ingram Content Group UK Ltd.
Pitfield, Milton Keynes, MK11 3LW, UK
UKHW020305070725
460420UK00018B/177